Best Foliage Shrubs

Stefan Buczacki
Best Foliage Shrubs

HAMLYN

Executive Art Editor Robin Whitecross
Executive Editor Anna Mumford
Designer Michael Whitehead
Editors Emily Wright and Selina Higgins
Production Alison Myer
Picture Research Jenny Faithfull

First published in Great Britain in 1994
by Hamlyn an imprint of Reed Consumer Books Limited
Michelin House, 81 Fulham Road, London SW3 6RB
and Auckland, Melbourne, Singapore and Toronto

Reprinted 1994

Produced by Butler & Tanner
Printed in Frome, Somerset

ISBN 0 600 57735 X

A catalogue of this book is available at the British Library

CONTENTS

INTRODUCTION 6
  Leaves – Form and Function 8
  Foliage Shrubs in the Garden 10
  Food and Water 12
  Soil 13
  Pruning and Propagation 14
  Pests and Diseases 16

PLANT DIRECTORY
  Foliage Shrubs 20
  Conifers 120

Index 126
Photograph Acknowledgements 128
Temperature Chart 128

INTRODUCTION

Much as I love flowers, I am still saddened when I hear gardeners talk of them as if they were the sum total of the pleasure and beauty that gardens can offer. We forget too often that garden plants have leaves too. And I am reminded of the remarks made to me some years ago by one of the greatest modern garden designers, John Brookes, whose work I admire enormously. I was interviewing him for a television programme and asked what relative weight he accorded in his garden design philosophy to flowers and to foliage. Without hesitation, he said that foliage wins every time. A flower lasts on average, he explained, for about three weeks. Leaves are there for months on end, and indeed, if the plant is an evergreen, there is foliage present for the entire year.

So foliage should create the background, the carpet, upon which the flowers are placed. And it must be admitted that there are relatively few garden situations in which, no matter how dramatic the flowers, foliage isn't also visible. I suppose the most obvious must be some of the formal 'public park' bedding schemes in which massively flowered bedding plants with tiny leaves are planted so close together that the foliage itself is of no account. But even there, I don't doubt that such a planting will be counterbalanced by another close by in which the leaves of the plants take pride of place; and let's not forget that in the classic Victorian carpet bedding, it was leaves alone that provided the colour, the flowers themselves being clipped off.

In a temperate climate, however, the visual appearance of plants varies enormously from one season to another and there are precious few bedding plants tough enough to survive the winter and precious few herbaceous perennials that are reliably evergreen. The foliage present in the winter garden is largely the foliage of those plants with a permanent, woody, aboveground framework: the trees and the shrubs. But whilst most gardens are not big enough for more than one or two trees, shrubs are a very different matter. I have said on many occasions that

Foliage is the mainstay of any permanent planting

I consider shrubs the most important single type of plant in the modern garden because of their general ease of cultivation, the variety they offer in overall size and form, flower colour and size, flowering season and, of course, their leaves. And so I have absolutely no difficulty whatsoever in devoting a complete book to the shrub as a foliage plant.

Indeed, in selecting the species and varieties to include, I have even surprised myself when I realized how many must be left out. I have made my selection first, therefore, of those shrubs for which the foliage is the only important feature, the flowers and fruits being insignificant or non-existent. I have then chosen those types which have superb foliage as their greatest merit but which also have attractive flowers and/or fruit. And I have appreciated that there are, in reality, rather few major shrub groups for which flowers and foliage are of equal importance. I have tried moreover to be even-handed in my selection of evergreen and deciduous types to ensure that there will be interest and variety through the 12 months of the year.

A group of colourful foliage shrubs can be every bit as interesting as a floral planting

LEAVES – FORM AND FUNCTION

There are plants that manage without roots, finding other means to support themselves and other means to obtain water and mineral nutrients. There are plants without stems, preferring to spend their lives very close to soil level. There are plants without flowers, managing to reproduce themselves by vegetative means. But there are very, very few plants without leaves; and even among those that do exist, almost all have stems so modified in form and function as to appear leaf-like to the uninitiated. So, why are leaves so important; and why indeed are they so varied in shape and size?

For outstanding autumnal colour, few small shrubs beat the berberis

THE FUNCTION OF LEAVES

The importance of leaves can be summed up very simply: they are the principle organs for photosynthesis, the process by which the raw materials of water and carbon dioxide from the air are combined to form more complex chemicals known as carbohydrates, which serve both as food for the plant and the basis for its structural growth. The energy for the chemical reaction comes from sunlight but the essential ingredient that enables the reaction to take place is the chemical chlorophyll. Chlorophyll is green and its presence in the cells is the reason why most leaves are green. (The fact that a disproportionate number of the leaves depicted in this book are of some other colour will be explained shortly.)

But leaves have other functions, too. The most important is to provide the channel through which water is lost to the air by evaporation, this process in turn exerting a pull that draws more water up the plant from the roots, carrying mineral nutrients from the soil in the process. To photosynthesize most effectively, the leaf must present as large a surface area as possible to the sun. But the more sunlight a leaf receives, the more warmth it receives too, and consequently more water will evaporate from it. The danger, of course, is that water will be lost at a faster rate than the roots are able to take it up and the plant will wilt and possibly die as a result. Most of the features of leaves (apart from colour) that we find appealing are the leaves' attempts to limit water loss, whilst still obtaining as much sunlight as possible in their particular environment.

So perhaps this is a good moment to consider the different features of leaves, why they are as they are, and how they contribute to the overall appeal of the shrub.

LEAF COLOUR

Chlorophyll is green and so most leaves are green, but this green coloration is often masked, most attractively, by other colours. In purple or reddish leaves, coloured by pigments called anthocyanins, the chlorophyll seems to function no less efficiently and this particular colour variation occurs very widely in plants of many different families and groups – witness the numerous varieties called 'Purpurea' or 'Rubra'. In other plants, it is the yellow pigments known as carotenoids that mask the chlorophyll, giving rise to golden or yellow leaves and varieties called 'Aurea' or 'Lutea'. No-one seems to know how such variations evolved and, in many instances, it's hard to see a reason for them; but we should be grateful, nonetheless, for purple and yellow-foliaged plants are particularly valuable in garden design.

But, from an aesthetic point of view, it isn't the month after month leaf colour that is most important; it is the colour change that takes place in the leaves of many deciduous shrubs in autumn, just before they drop. Autumn colour alone is a factor that dictates the choice of many foliage shrubs, but whilst some genera such as *Acer* or *Fothergilla* are rightly renowned for their autumn colours, there are others in which it is less appreciated and I shall draw particular attention to them in the individual plant entries.

Many of the shrub varieties that I recommend are called 'Variegata' and they are characterized by leaves that have a spotted or marbled pattern in which discrete areas lack a green colour and, instead, are white or yellowish. In some instances, this effect is known to be caused by virus contamination of the tissues – virus that is transmitted from parent plant to progeny in cuttings but is not usually passed on in the seed. In other cases, however, the cause of the variegation is unknown but it almost invariably confers some reduced vigour on the plant. Presumably, this is because the lack of part of their chlorophyll means that they function less efficiently and so grow more

slowly. In shady conditions, variegated plants sometimes revert to producing all-green leaves and many variegated shrubs, even in normal sunny positions, may produce shoots bearing only green foliage. These should always be cut off.

The colour of leaves may be enhanced by a glossy coating and this is brought about by the presence of natural waxes which are intended to reduce water loss through the surface. Glossy leaves are often a feature of plants that grow in very hot conditions, where evaporation rates will be high; or conversely, in very cold ones where the soil is frozen for part of the year and almost no water can then be taken up through the roots. Another mechanism to reduce water loss is the presence of hairs on the leaf surface and, when they are in large numbers, they give a markedly silvery and extremely attractive effect. But because such hairs trap moisture (which would ultimately result in

rotting), they tend to be confined to plants from warm climates only and so are a characteristic feature of species from the Mediterranean.

LEAF SHAPE

The shape of leaves can be almost infinitely variable, embracing the elongated, inwardly rolled needles of a conifer or a rosemary, through the more or less rounded, oval or elongated shapes of a prunus, laurel or box; the lobed, indented or divided leaves of an acer or sorbus to the finely dissected, almost fern-like foliage of an artemisia. All of these are yet more manifestations of that compromise between enhancing light capture and limiting water loss, of balancing surface area against volume. Consider leaf shape when choosing planting positions. For example, no plant with a thin, fragile, finely divided leaf is likely to survive for long in the full force of the sun. Conversely, a plant like a holly, in which at least part of the leaf is so reduced as to exist only as a spine, is likely to be a pretty tough customer.

LEAF SIZE

And so, finally, to leaf size. Like shape, this varies enormously, and in this book, I think the extremes are represented by some of the tiny needles of junipers or other conifers, and the immense, majestic-looking leaves of *Rhododendron sinogrande*. Size, of course, is linked with shape in reflecting leaf function but there is a very practical aspect to size in garden planning. In small gardens, plants with abnormally large leaves will almost never look right; and if the leaves are not only abnormally large but also deciduous, your garden will all but disappear beneath a leafy carpet every autumn.

Foliage can be simple in shape or more complex, as seen in these rue leaves

FOLIAGE SHRUBS IN THE GARDEN

I have already referred to shrubs, in general, as probably the most important plants in the modern garden. And, although I am open to understandable arguments from the flowering shrub fraternity, I'm not sure that the foliage shrub isn't the most valuable, or at least, the most versatile of all. The question to ask oneself is how to best use them within the overall design of a garden. Should they be grown alone or integrated with each other, with flowering shrubs, herbaceous perennials, annuals or bulbs? And the answer is, 'Yes', to all of the above.

Let's first consider the foliage shrub as an isolated specimen. By and large, an evergreen makes the best choice here, particularly in a small garden for, although many deciduous species are pretty enough even when leafless, they would need to be rather remarkable to hold your interest throughout the winter months. By contrast, in a larger garden, a deciduous species, especially one with winter flowers, can be effective as an isolated specimen if there is plenty of evergreen interest in other areas of the garden. But any such specimen shrub must be positioned prominently and, although the most obvious spot is within a lawn, it can also be placed in a gravelled area, in a gap between paving slabs or blocks or even, provided the plant isn't too large, in a container. Indeed, I do wish that people would be a little more adventurous in using isolated specimen shrubs within a 'hard' area. To my mind, there is nothing else that sets off the effect of foliage as well as materials such as gravel or stone chippings.

CHOOSING FOLIAGE SHRUBS

Generally foliage shrubs blend very well with each other, and, unlike some flowers, there are very few leaf colours so strong and strident as to produce unpleasant clashes when they are juxtaposed. So on this score, most types will look attractive alongside most others. Where I do feel care is needed, however, is in producing a blend of leaf sizes and shapes, especially where the more individual or unusual shapes are concerned. Some foliage forms (yuccas and fatsias are perhaps the most obvious), for instance, generally lend themselves much better to the formal type of garden rather than to the more casual and traditional one. A mixture of evergreen and deciduous types will usually produce the most satisfactory effect although, in a large enough garden, a bed devoted, for example, to shrubs selected solely for their autumn colour can be stunningly appealing.

PLANTING CONSIDERATIONS

Where foliage shrubs are mixed with flowering shrubs, a decision must be taken on whether they are to play an equal or a subordinate role. The latter is easier to plan for, simply creating an

Fatsias are useful shrubs for containers and add a touch of exotica

Rosemary, berberis and hebe in a mixed border planting

attractive background of colour and form against which the flowers are displayed to best effect. Use the leaves of the foliage shrubs to supplement those of the flowering plants themselves. Where the foliage shrubs are to have importance equal to that of the flowering species, however, the same considerations apply as when a mix of different flowers is being planned. Consideration must be given to colour, size and period of greatest interest; a foliage shrub chosen for its autumn effect, for example, is not best positioned alongside a shrub that flowers at the same time, especially if its flowers don't blend agreeably with the reds and golds of autumn leaves.

For an average-sized mixed border, combine foliage and flowering shrubs for best effect. A blend of two or three of each, of differing sizes, will create a year-round framework to be dressed by the herbaceous perennials in summer, but it is important to select shrubs that will themselves be of winter interest. The whole purpose of having shrubs in the border fails if they can't

take over the appeal with the onset of autumn and the dying down of the herbaceous plants.

Bulbs blend well with foliage shrubs of almost all kinds but I find they offer their greatest value when a few early-flowering forms are planted beneath

deciduous species because they will put on an attractive show before the shrubs themselves have come into leaf. It's important when planting bulbs beneath evergreen shrubs to choose those relatively few types that are tolerant both of some shade and also of the dryness that will almost inevitably exist there.

In many ways I feel that annuals mix with foliage shrubs less obviously and less satisfactorily than with other types of plants. Visually, this is because their colours are often rather strident and difficult to blend, but from a cultivation standpoint, the soil disturbance that the planting and removal of annuals involves will usually be to the detriment of healthy shrubs. For both of these reasons, annuals in fairly subdued colours that freely self-sow, such as violets and forget-me-nots, work particularly well.

DECIDUOUS OR EVERGREEN?

Whether a shrub is deciduous or evergreen is immensely important in the garden. Will it have leaves all year round or just for six or seven months? At first sight, it may appear that an evergreen species will always offer the best return, but there are other less obvious considerations. Might not a shrub whose leaves and branches always appear the same be somewhat boring, especially if it doesn't have interesting flowers or fruit? The very existence of seasonal changes in deciduous species, from the first opening of fresh green buds in spring right through to the colour changes that precede autumn leaf fall, are appealing enough in themselves, almost irrespective of any intrinsic appeal that the summer foliage offers. And once the leaves have fallen, the bare twigs may have an engaging colour or texture to maintain interest.

Undeniably, if it is permanent screening or privacy that you require, then an evergreen shrub will be your almost invariable choice. Nonetheless, the evergreen will cast shade all year round and is more likely to be damaged by winter snow, although it can begin growth more rapidly in the spring, without having to wait for buds to swell and burst. But a garden of evergreens alone can be a rather dispiriting spectacle and I would always urge any garden plan, be it of a dedicated shrubbery, a mixed border or a group of specimen plants, to include both deciduous and evergreen species.

FOOD AND WATER

No foliage shrub will give you satisfaction if its foliage isn't lush and vigorous. And as I have explained already, the importance of the leaves means that a plant with vigorous, actively growing foliage will be a good, vigorous and active plant overall. So whilst feeding is of great importance, it needn't take up much of your time and, once established, shrubs require relatively little annual attention; a once-a-season application of fertilizer and a twice-a-year application of mulch are ideal. But let's be honest; many make do with less than that, yet still produce the goods.

It helps, nonetheless, to realize that each plant nutrient has a different effect and benefit and, to put it simply, of the three major substances, nitrogen (N) encourages leafy growth, potash (K) encourages fruiting and flowering and phosphate (P) encourages root development. Of course, it's misleading to try to look at each in isolation, but logic suggests that a plant being grown mainly for its foliage would benefit most from nitrogen. And nitrogen really is the key element so it must be present in any fertilizer that is applied and I feel that, for foliage shrubs, a balanced general blend is best. The fact that it is described as 'balanced' means that the formulation is centred on the amount of nitrogen and that the amounts of phosphate and potash have been chosen accordingly.

CHOOSING A FERTILIZER

There are two alternative fertilizers of this general balanced type: the organically-based fish, blood and bone with an approximate N:P:K ratio of 5:5:6, or artificial mixtures such as Growmore with a ratio of 7:7:7, although I find the artificials to be rather too fast-acting for optimum results and their benefits don't last very long. It's worth a reminder that proprietary fish, blood and bone with the above composition is only organically based, not entirely

Mineral deficiency on foliage

organic as many organic gardeners seem to believe. This is because a mixture comprising only fish meal, dried blood and bone meal would be deficient in potash, so potassium sulphate is added to produce a more useful blend. Fertilizers such as these should be applied at a rate of around 70 grams per square metre (2oz per square yard) which, in practice, means a small handful scattered around each plant.

If your foliage shrub has equal or at least significant importance as a flowering plant, you can make do with a general fertilizer but you will usually obtain better results with one that contains proportionally more potash to encourage flowering. I use proprietary rose fertilizer, of which there are now organic and artificial types; these should also be applied at about 70 grams per square metre (2oz per square yard).

Bear in mind that there's little to be gained by simply applying dry fertilizer powder around a shrub growing in dry soil for it will remain on the surface, become caked and be of no benefit to the plant. Ideally, it should be applied after rain, raked into the soil surface and also then be watered in with a watering can or hose.

MULCHING

In order to try to maintain the soil around your shrubs in a moist condition, a mulch should be applied in spring and again in autumn. But do remember that the soil must be wet initially – a mulch will keep a dry soil dry just as much as it will a wet one wet. By and large, the most useful mulching material is home-produced garden compost or leaf mould but some plants will fare better with well-rotted manure (I have indicated where this is so in the individual descriptions) and a few, acid-loving types benefit from a mulch of chopped conifer needles.

SOIL

Good soil is the key to success with all types of plants, foliage or not. But all good soil isn't the same – there can be a good organic acidic soil just as there can be a good free-draining alkaline loam. Some plants will be more successful in one than the other and I have indicated in the individual descriptions which is most appropriate for which. Because of this, it is important to understand the make-up of your own garden soil and appreciate the relative importance of different features of it.

Aucubas are tolerant of both extremely dry soil and heavy clay

THE COMPOSITION OF SOIL

There are four main solid ingredients to any soil: the mineral particles, which are divided, in decreasing size, into sand, silt and clay, and the organic matter or humus. In addition, of course, there are the more transient, non-solid components: water and air. Because of the unique physical properties of the minute particles that make up clay, this is perhaps the key substance, and a soil with a high clay content will be slow to warm up in spring but then retains warmth well and is likely to be generously supplied with nutrients. In dry conditions it can be hard and impenetrable whereas in wet winter weather, it may become waterlogged. By contrast, a light sandy soil will warm up quickly, cool down quickly, and being free-draining, will lose water and nutrients rapidly. Humus (part-decomposed organic matter) will improve both types of soil for it contains natural gel-like substances that bind together soil particles to form crumbs and also help the retention of moisture by their sponge-like properties. Always dig in plenty of compost, manure or other organic matter before planting.

ACIDITY AND ALKALINITY

There's another aspect of your garden soil that you may need to take account of with many types of shrub: its relative acidity or alkalinity, usually expressed as the pH on a scale from 0 to 14. Soils with a pH above 7 are alkaline, those with a pH below 7, acid. Most soils are naturally somewhere between about pH 6 and pH 7.5 (more or less neutral) and most shrubs will thrive in these conditions. But there are numerous exceptions. Rhododendrons and pieris are among the many types that must have an acidic soil and it's true that many others will survive but survive rather inadequately if the soil is too far on the alkaline side of neutral.

The pH of a slightly acid soil can be raised fairly simply by adding lime but there are few shrubs that will benefit greatly from this. A strongly acid soil is unlikely to be changed to any significant degree and unfortunately, the procedure that would be very valuable, that of enabling gardeners to decrease the pH of a naturally alkaline soil, is also extremely difficult to do – although companies selling sulphur as a soil additive for this purpose might try to persuade you otherwise.

Spiraea will grow in most soils

PRUNING AND PROPAGATION

With rather few exceptions (the use of foliage shrubs to form hedges being the most obvious) pruning is probably less important overall with foliage shrubs than it is with most other types of garden plants. Unlike climbers, fruit trees, roses or even flowering shrubs, a plant grown predominantly for its foliage will generally perform pretty well with almost no routine attention. Nonetheless, performance (by which I mean the production of fresh new shoots bearing fresh new foliage) will sometimes be enhanced by pruning and, to this end, it's worth looking rather more closely at what the operation entails. Likewise, propagation of foliage shrubs is not seen by some gardeners as a necessary task. Surely, the reasoning goes, you are unlikely to want many more of these plants than you have already? Such an attitude ignores two of the greatest pleasures of gardening: sharing your plants with others and the rewarding experience of simply taking that cutting and nurturing a plant to maturity.

Pruning promotes plant growth

WHY PRUNE?

Pruning involves cutting off parts of plants. Clearly, this reduces their size but, more importantly, it stimulates other parts to grow. The buds at the end or apex of a stem exert a chemical-suppressing influence on other buds further down. This phenomenon is called apical dominance. Cut off the end of a stem, therefore, and those other buds, freed of chemical constraint, will burst into life. If they are leaf buds, you will have foliage further down the stem. Sometimes, some pruning away of the apex is usefully combined with simply bending the stem down to the horizontal, since this helps to diminish apical dominance and stimulate more uniform foliage production.

Cutting away a large proportion of a plant is called hard pruning; cutting away a little is called light pruning. Generally speaking, you should hard prune those plants that are the less vigorous growers. The reason for this is simply because in stimulating bud development as I've described, pruning actually generates more growth. So the harder you prune, the more you will have to prune and if you regularly clip a vigorous hedge such as privet, the more you will have to clip.

HOW TO PRUNE

Regardless of the amount of stem to be removed, pruning cuts should always be made just above a bud, leaf, flower, branch fork or other actively growing structure, never in the middle of a stem or branch. This ensures that the cut surface heals quickly and doesn't merely wither and allow decay organisms to enter. On other than very slender stems, the cut should be sloped away from the bud or other organ, but must not be so close as to damage it – about 5mm (¼in) above is generally safe. And even on large woody stems, never apply a wound-sealing compound. These were once considered a benefit but are now thought at best

Box can be clipped into a variety of shapes for a decorative effect

useless and at worst positively harmful. With plants being grown for their foliage alone, the time of pruning is not critical but, in general, you will see that I advise doing it in the spring. This is so that the wounds will heal quickly and new growth will follow with little delay. If the shrub also has flowering appeal, then this is an important factor and pruning should always follow, not precede flowering if the flower buds are not to be removed.

TOOLS FOR PRUNING

Good pruning is best achieved with good tools, and no gardener can manage without a pair of secateurs or pruners. Choose between the single-bladed anvil pattern which are best for hard woody stems but tend to crush softer ones, and the two-bladed scissor or by-pass type which are less robust but more gentle in action. Ideally, have both. If you have large shrubs with stout woody stems, you will also require a pair of loppers which, in essence, are long-handled secateurs for thicker branches and are also available in both anvil or by-pass style. You may occasionally need to resort to something stronger still and a curved pruning saw may be necessary on really big and tough shrubs that verge on tree size. As with all garden tools, I can do no more than repeat my oft-given advice – buy the best that you can afford, and remember that the difference between good and poor quality cutting tools is more marked than with most other types of gardening aid.

PROPAGATION

While propagation of foliage shrubs is very rarely essential, it is always rewarding and so I have included brief notes on the best methods under the individual descriptions. The various propagation options are outlined below.

Cuttings: Apart from hardwood cuttings, all types should be rooted (or 'struck', to use the gardening term) in a covered chamber, either a small heated propagator or a covered cold frame. It is very important to maintain a moist atmosphere around the cuttings otherwise they will lose water through their leaves at a time when, lacking roots, they are unable to replace it from below. Even with a covered propagator, therefore, you should pay careful attention to the moisture content of the rooting medium and use a hand sprayer to mist over the cuttings regularly. The cold frame can also be used for hardwood cuttings although I prefer to root these in a sheltered spot in the open garden, inserting the shoots in a narrow 'V'-shaped trench in the bottom of which I have layered some sand. The effectiveness of the type of

Taking cuttings using a sharp knife

A propagator full of rooted cuttings

medium (sand, soil-based compost and so forth) into which the cuttings are placed varies from one type of plant to another, and I have given my suggestions in each of the plant descriptions. In general, cuttings of all types should be removed from the parent plant with a clean cut made just below a bud. using a sharp knife

Layering: Evergreen shrubs can present problems, for even if cuttings are taken during their dormant season in the conventional hardwood manner, the presence of leaves means that water will still be lost at a time when the plant has no means of replacing it. The difficulty can often be overcome by layering – anchoring a stem into the soil whilst it is still attached to the parent plant. The disadvantage is that some patience is needed as layerings rarely root satisfactorily in less than about 18 months.

Growing from seed: Propagating from seed is covered in full in *Best Climbers*, Book I in the series.

PESTS AND DISEASES

In common with every other type of garden plant, foliage shrubs are prone to pests and diseases, but no more so, in general. Certainly, they are less prone to the problems that attack soft and fleshy tissues and to which fruit, vegetables and annuals are especially subject. As an indication of their relative significance, whilst I only advocate the use of chemical controls on any plant as a last rather than a first resort, I think it's probably true that I use even less pesticidal chemicals on my foliage shrubs than on any other individual plant group. But it always helps to understand the opposition and their objectives before dealing with any difficulty they might cause.

PESTS

Pests all belong to the animal kingdom, although biologically they are no different from their non-pest relatives and it's simply because their preferred food happens to be our garden plants that we give them a special title. They range in size from mammals such as deer, rabbits, mice and voles, through birds to insects, both big and small, and mites, which are small or truly minute. While mammals and birds, of course, are warm-blooded and more or less equally active all year round (apart from those mammals that hibernate), both insects and mites are cold-blooded and so their activity and reproductive rate speed up as the temperature rises – so they are especially important in the summer. Insect pests can be divided roughly into two groups: the sap-sucking types, such as aphids,

Viburnum suffering from blackfly

whiteflies and scale insects, which achieve much of their impact through force of numbers, gradually wearing down a plant's vigour; and the chewing types, such as caterpillars and beetles, that may be small in quantity but are rather large in effect for they remove pieces bodily. On foliage shrubs, where the leaves are the real object of our gardening efforts, anything that bodily eats pieces of leaf is bound to have a major impact.

DISEASES

Diseases are caused most importantly by microscopic fungi: mildews and rusts and leaf spots are very familiar examples. Like many pests, they flourish best in relatively warm and sheltered conditions so shrubs growing close together in a shrubbery are more at risk than those standing alone as isolated specimens. All fungi require moisture for their spores to germinate and grow but, contrary to what is sometimes thought, not all require damp conditions thereafter, the most important example of this being the type called powdery mildews. After their initial germination, mildews thrive best in hot, dry conditions.

A few diseases on foliage shrubs may be caused by viruses, usually introduced into the plant's tissues by aphids or other sap-sucking pests. The effects are much more indefinite than those of fungal diseases and often take the form of crinkling or crumpling of the leaves, indefinite leaf mottling and sometimes overall feeble growth although it usually requires an expert to distinguish between these effects and those arising from other causes, such as inadequate feeding. In one or two instances, rather attractive and desirable effects are created as a result of virus infection and, as I indicate on p.9, the leaf patterning on several variegated varieties is brought about by the presence of virus in the tissues.

TREATMENT

Knowing what we do about how pests and diseases thrive, what can be done to minimize their effects? The ideal solution would be to choose shrub species and varieties that have natural resistance but, in practice, this is very rarely feasible. Unlike food crops, no-one has attempted to breed shrub varieties solely for this purpose and such resistance as does exist (*Vinca minor* is resistant to rust, for example, whereas *V. major* is susceptible) is mere chance. But it's also worth saying that the reason no-one has deemed resistance breeding to be worthwhile is largely because pests and diseases have relatively little impact on foliage shrubs. A second approach is to create an environment less attractive to the pests and diseases, but apart from the difference between shrubs growing in the open as opposed to being hemmed in

SYMPTOMS ON LEAVES		

PROBLEM	DETAIL	PROBABLE CAUSE
Wilting	General	Short of water
		Root pest, or disease
		Wilt disease
Holed	Generally ragged	Small pests (millepedes, woodlice)
		Capsid bugs
	Elongate holes; usually with slime present	Slugs or snails
	Fairly large holes over entire leaf or confined to edges	Caterpillars Beetles Birds
Discoloured	Black	Sooty mould
	Predominantly red	Short of water
	More or less bleached	Fertilizer deficiency
		Short of water
		Too much water
	Irregular yellowish patterns	Virus (but check that not a variegated variety)
	Irregular tunnels	Leaf miners
	Surface flecking	Leaf hoppers
	Brown (scorched) in spring	Frost
Spotted	Brown-black, irregular, no mould	Leaf spot
	Small, dusty, brown, black or bright yellow-orange coloured	Rust
Mouldy	Black	Sooty mould
	Grey, fluffy	Grey mould
	White (or rarely brown), velvety	Mildew
Infested with insects	White, moth-like, tiny	Whiteflies
	Green, grey, black or other colour	Aphids
	Flat, encrusted, like limpets	Scale insects
	Large, six legs, worm-like	Caterpillars
Cobwebs present	Leaves also discoloured	Red spider mites

SYMPTOMS ON FLOWERS		

PROBLEM	DETAIL	PROBABLE CAUSE
Drooping	General	Short of water
		End of flowering period
Tattered	Lots of tiny holes	Caterpillars
	Large pieces torn away	Birds
Removed entirely	Usually discarded nearby	Birds
Discoloured	Powdery white covering	Mildew
Mouldy	Fluffy grey mould	Grey mould

SYMPTOMS ON STEMS OR BRANCHES		

PROBLEM	DETAIL	PROBABLE CAUSE
Eaten through	On young plants	Slugs or snails
	On older plants	Mice, voles, rabbits
Infested with insects	Green, grey, black or other colour	Aphids
	Flat, encrusted, like limpets	Scale insects
	Large, six legs, worm-like	Caterpillars
Rotten	At base, young plants	Stem and foot rot
	On mature shrubs	Decay fungus
Blister on stems	More or less spherical	Gall
	Target-like	Canker
Dying back	General	Short of water
		Canker or coral spot
		Root pest or disease

PESTS AND DISEASES

The effects of sooty mould on ivy

by other vegetation, it is difficult to take much practical advantage of this.

A third approach is to keep watch carefully for the initial signs of attack early in the season and then physically nip off the problem. Certainly, pinching out small aphid colonies or the shoot tips carrying the first tell-tale whitening of mildew in the spring will delay the onset of serious damage and is to be encouraged. But it will seldom be the complete answer and it is then that more direct action is needed. And it is then, too, that personal choice becomes important.

No gardener these days can fail to appreciate that over-use of chemicals in the garden will cause harm to the environment. Very few chemicals can discriminate between good and harmful insects, some have unfortunate side-effects on other organisms (some insecticides, for example, are harmful to fish) and yet others may persist in the soil with rather uncertain long-term consequences. I must emphasize that these effects are at least as likely to be brought about by so-called natural or organic products as they are by artificial ones. My advice, therefore, is only to use any chemical in moderation; to use it as the last, not the first, option; and, of course, to use it only in the manner and at the doses that the manufacturers indicate.

I have listed the most common and important garden fungicides and insecticides and also given a key to the most frequent problems likely to be found on foliage shrubs, together with my suggested treatments. Because fertilizer deficiency can sometimes cause rather dramatic foliage effects, I have also included for convenience the commonest of the symptoms likely to arise from this cause. Although my primary interest in this book is the leaf, I have inevitably also included some examples of the flower, stem and branch problems that affect foliage shrubs (see p.17).

SOME FUNGICIDES, INSECTICIDES AND PESTICIDAL CHEMICALS USEFUL FOR CONTROLLING PROBLEMS ON FOLIAGE SHRUBS

FUNGICIDES	USES AND COMMENTS
Benomyl Carbendazim Thiophanate-methyl	Systemic, for most foliage and stem diseases, including mildew and grey mould
Myclobutanil	Systemic, especially useful for leaf spots and rust
Propiconazole	Systemic, especially useful for leaf spots and rust
Sulphur*	Non-systemic, many foliage diseases
Triforine	Systemic, many foliage diseases

INSECTICIDES	USES AND COMMENTS
Derris*	Contact, most pests
Dimethoate	Systemic, most pests
Natural soaps*	Contact, most pests
Permethrin	Contact, most pests
Phoxim	Contact, soil pests
Pirimicarb	Contact, specific to aphids

INSECTICIDES	USES AND COMMENTS
Pyrethrum*	Contact, most pests
Tar oil	Contact, use in dormant season only on deciduous shrubs to kill overwintering pests on bark

SLUG AND SNAIL KILLERS	USES AND COMMENTS
Metaldehyde	As pellets, mini-pellets or liquid
Methiocarb	As pellets

*Generally acceptable to organic gardeners
Systemic substances are absorbed by the plant and so require less frequent and less accurate spraying than contact materials

Note: It should be noted that some of these chemicals are only available in particular formulations or in combination with certain other chemicals. Some may also be marketed for specific pest or disease problems only. In every case, you must read the label directions carefully to be sure that the product is being used for the purpose and in the manner for which it is intended. The names given above are those of the active chemical ingredients. These will not be the same as the product names but will be found printed on the product label.

TREATMENTS FOR COMMON PEST AND DISEASE PROBLEMS ON FOLIAGE SHRUBS

PROBLEM	TREATMENT
Aphids	Use any proprietary contact insecticide; pick off affected shoots by hand or wash off insects with hose.
Beetles	Normally, treatment is not necessary or justified but in cases of extensive attack use any proprietary contact insecticide
Birds	Erect netting or other protection; in really severe cases, erect bird scarers but remember that all birds enjoy legal protection and may not be harmed
Canker	Cut out and destroy affected branches; no chemical treatment is possible
Capsid bugs	The insects are too unpredictable and erratic in occurrence to make any treatment feasible
Caterpillars	Pick off by hand if the caterpillars can be found and are present in small numbers. If masses of insects occur, pick off and destroy entire affected leaves or use any proprietary contact insecticide
Coral spot	Cut away and destroy affected branches or twigs, cutting well into the healthy wood. On very valuable foliage shrubs, spray the surrounding branches with a systemic fungicide
Fertilizer deficiency	Give general balanced liquid fertilizer
Fungal decay	Cut out and destroy affected parts; no other treatment is feasible
Gall	Normally no treatment is justified but cut out if severely disfiguring
Grey mould	Destroy affected parts; spray with systemic fungicide.
Leaf hoppers	The insects are too erratic and unpredictable to make any treatment practicable
Leaf miners	Remove and destroy affected leaves on herbaceous plants
Leaf spot	In most instances no treatment is necessary for leaf spot diseases are rarely severe. Where attacks appear to be related to general poor growth, however, spray with systemic fungicide
Mice	Set traps or use proprietary poison baits
Mildew	Ensure that plants are not allowed to become too dry and apply systemic fungicide or sulphur

PROBLEM	TREATMENT
Millepedes	Dust affected area with derris
Rabbits	The only sure protection is by using a wire netting fence with the lower edge turned outwards at 90° over the soil surface
Red spider mites	No treatment is really feasible although keeping plants well watered and mulched will help limit the impact of attacks
Root pests	Normally, no treatment is feasible but with severe and persistent attacks, dust around affected plants with derris or other soil insecticide
Root disease	Destroy severely affected plants
Rust	Spray with propiconazole fungicide
Scale insects	Spray or drench with systemic insecticide
Slugs	Use proprietary slug pellets or liquid controls or home-made remedies such as traps baited with beer. Surround the base of plants with fine powders such as ash or soot or a low barrier of finely spiny twigs such as gorse
Snails	If serious, use methods recommended for slugs but generally they are less serious and fewer in number and can be combated by collecting them by hand and by locating them and eradicating them from their hiding places
Sooty mould	Wash off mould with water or destroy badly affected leaves and then identify and treat the insect pest responsible for forming the honeydew on which the mould grows
Stem and foot rot	Little can be done but as it is often associated with waterlogging, improve drainage of the affected area
Virus	Effects are usually mild, so no treatment is necessary (see also my comments on p. 9)
Voles	Set mouse traps or use proprietary poison baits
Whiteflies	No treatment is feasible on outdoor plants
Wilt disease	No treatment is very effective but drench surrounding soil with systemic fungicide
Woodlice	Dust around plants with proprietary soil insecticide and locate them and eradicate them from their hiding places

ABUTILON

Abutilon megapotamicum

❝ Abutilons are relatives of the mallows in the family Malvaceae and, as befits plants from the tropics and sub-tropics, most are species for the conservatory rather than the open garden in all except the mildest areas. Abutilon megapotamicum is no exception and it is so lax a shrub that it is almost better described as a short climber, for it always needs some support. But in its variegated form, especially, it is a distinctly pretty thing and well worthy of being grown in a sheltered spot. As in its tender relative, A. pictum 'Thompsonii', the variegation arises from virus infection (p.16). ❞

FOLIAGE INTEREST
Evergreen, dark green, oval with more or less heart-shaped base.
NON-FOLIAGE APPEAL
Strikingly pretty, small, bell-shaped, red and orange flowers throughout the summer.
SUITABILITY AS HEDGING
None.
SITE AND SOIL
Sheltered from wind and hot sun, ideally against the wall of a building, in rich, fertile, well-drained soil.
HARDINESS
Barely hardy, tolerating 0 to -5°C (32 to 23°F).
SIZE
About 1 x 1m (3 x 3ft) after three years, 2 x 2m (6 x 6ft) ultimately.

CARE
Mulch lightly in autumn and early spring and give a balanced rose or general fertilizer in spring.

PROPAGATION
By softwood cuttings in late spring or semi-ripe cuttings in summer in a rather humus-rich, soil-based compost in a cold frame or in a propagator with slight bottom heat. The normal species also by seed in spring but the variegated form does not come true. Harden off plants fully before planting out.

A. megapotamicum 'Variegatum'

PRUNING
Not necessary, but straggly plants will regenerate and become more bushy if cut back lightly in spring.

PROBLEMS
Whiteflies, red spider mites, aphids and scale insects.

RECOMMENDED VARIETIES
'Variegatum' has an irregular yellowish leaf mosaic.

Abutilon vitifolium

❝ This attractive South American shrub is sometimes listed as Corynabutilon. This may make it harder to find in catalogues but this shouldn't deter you for, while it is generally promoted as a large, flowering shrub, its large, vine-like leaves make it a valuable foliage plant too, especially in mild areas where it may retain most of the leaves through the winter. ❞

FOLIAGE INTEREST
Deciduous or semi-evergreen, large, grapevine-shaped, greyish-green leaves, yellowish in autumn.
NON-FOLIAGE APPEAL
Large, open cup-shaped pale lavender flowers.
SUITABILITY AS HEDGING
None.
SITE AND SOIL
Full sun with shelter from cold winds, in almost any soil although best on rich organic loams. Tends to perform badly on thinner and alkaline soils.
HARDINESS
Fairly hardy, tolerating around -5 to -10°C (23 to 14°F).
SIZE
Attains about 3 x 1m (10 x 3ft) after three years, about 6 x 3.5m (20 x 12ft) ultimately.

CARE
Mulch in autumn and early spring and give a balanced rose fertilizer in spring.
PROPAGATION
By softwood or semi-ripe cuttings in summer, rooted in a soil-based compost in a cold frame.

ACANTHOPANAX

PRUNING
None necessary.
PROBLEMS
None.

> **RECOMMENDED VARIETIES**
> There is nothing to choose between the available varieties in respect of foliage appeal, although the form *album* has particularly attractive white flowers.

Acanthopanax (syn. Eleutherococcus)

❝ *The family Araliaceae includes several valuable foliage shrubs, generally characterized by large, divided and glossy leaves. Fatsia (p.72) is probably the best known but the rather thorny plant still popularly known as Acanthopanax (but more correctly as Eleutherococcus) sieboldianus is another, too frequently neglected. Like others in the family, they have the distinct merit of looking much more tender than they are and so can bring a tropical feel to a small garden or courtyard planting, which is where I think they are really seen to best effect. They make good container subjects.* ❞

CARE
Mulch in autumn and in early spring, as well as giving a balanced general fertilizer in the spring.
PROPAGATION
Softwood cuttings in early summer or semi-ripe cuttings in late summer in a soil-based compost in a cold frame.

Acanthopanax sieboldianus **'Variegatus'**

FOLIAGE INTEREST
Deciduous, with usually five-lobed, toothed, pale green leaves each with a thorn at the base. Fairly good yellow autumn colour.
NON-FOLIAGE APPEAL
Small greenish-white flowers sometimes appear in early summer in good seasons, followed by spherical black fruits.
SUITABILITY AS HEDGING
None.

SITE AND SOIL Best in a sheltered spot, although the variegated form will lose its variegation in the shade, in rich, fertile, well-drained soil; use a good soil-based compost, such as John Innes No 3, in containers.
HARDINESS Hardy, tolerating -15 to -20°C (5 to -4°F).
SIZE About 1 x 1m (3 x 3ft) after three years, 2.5 x 2.5m (8 x 8ft) ultimately.

Also by careful division in spring, by removal of natural layers or by root cuttings in winter.
PRUNING
Not necessary, but may be cut back moderately hard in spring to encourage new leaf and shoot production.

> **RECOMMENDED VARIETIES**
> 'Variegatus' has cream-white leaf patterning, mostly confined to the margins.

PROBLEMS
None.

ACER Maple

The family Aceraceae contains only one genus of significance. But what a genus. As a group, *Acer* probably includes more plants with spectacular autumn leaf colour than any other. The genus is large, with around 150 species, mainly of small to medium-sized deciduous trees although there are some evergreen forms and, more importantly for present purposes, some smaller forms that may not be shrubs in the conventional sense but are so slow growing that they seldom reach tree size in most gardens. Not only are there many species of *Acer*, but many of them include large numbers of varieties for which demand often exceeds supply and your choice will, therefore, be restricted by what your supplier has available.

Acer ginnala (syn. *Acer tataricum ginnala*) Amur Maple

" This is a species with a wide distribution in the Far East and, although I have seen tree-sized specimens in gardens, it usually adopts a much-branched bushy habit without being pruned, that results in an attractive large shrub instead. It makes an ideal companion for larger acers and other autumn foliage plants in large gardens. "

FOLIAGE INTEREST
Deciduous, three-lobed, toothed leaves, yellow in spring, later mid-green, and bright red in autumn.

NON-FOLIAGE APPEAL
Whitish flowers in spring with clusters of brownish fruit which often stay on the plant well after the leaves have dropped.

SUITABILITY AS HEDGING
None.

SITE AND SOIL Most, unlike many maples, tolerant of wind and sun, but best in deep, fertile loams although tolerant of alkalinity.

HARDINESS Very hardy, tolerating at least -20°C (-4°F).

SIZE Generally up to about 5 x 5m (16 x 16ft) in gardens, although potentially a tree up to 10 x 8m (30 x 25ft).

RECOMMENDED VARIETIES
Normal species generally available, although selected forms, such as 'Fire' and 'Flame', with supposedly better leaf colour may occasionally be seen.

CARE
Mulch in autumn and early spring and give a balanced general fertilizer in spring, at least until well established.

PROPAGATION
From seed after stratifying in a sandy, soil-based compost over winter.

PRUNING
Not necessary and generally to be discouraged as, like all acers, it is prone to attack by coral spot (p.16) through damaged tissues.

PROBLEMS
Coral spot, decay fungi in wounds, scorching of foliage may occur in spring.

Acer ginnala

Acer japonicum
Japanese maple

❝ *There are few maples more lovely than this and although many other species originated in Japan, this is the one that is always known as the Japanese maple. You may now see some of the sub-species and varieties listed by the more taxonomically inclined nurseries as* Acer shirazawanum *but for me, the Japanese maple will always be* A. japonicum. *Both the true species and its variants are often seen and grown as much-branched large shrubs.* ❞

RECOMMENDED VARIETIES

The normal species is widely available but better for foliage appeal are 'Aureum' with butter yellow leaves, turning more golden in summer and red-orange in autumn; 'Aconitifolium' with highly divided, almost filigree foliage (and is often confused on that account with *Acer palmatum* 'Dissectum'), pale greyish-green in summer and with a blend of yellow, orange and red in autumn; 'Vitifolium' with large, fan-shaped leaves with mauves and purples in autumn.

CARE

Mulch in autumn and early spring and give a balanced general fertilizer in spring, at least until well established.

PROPAGATION

The true species from seed after stratifying in a sandy soil-based compost over winter. The varieties will not come true from seed and can only be

FOLIAGE INTEREST
Deciduous, many-lobed, toothed leaves, varying in colour with variety through the season but all with very good autumn colours.

NON-FOLIAGE APPEAL
Bunches of small, mainly reddish flowers in spring.

SUITABILITY AS HEDGING
None.

SITE AND SOIL
Best with some shelter from winds; the true species is tolerant of full sun but the paler-colour variants, especially 'Aureum', will be scorched. Most soils, but best in deep, fertile slightly acidic loams although tolerant of some alkalinity.

HARDINESS Very hardy, tolerating at least -20°C (-4°F) if sheltered from cold winds.

SIZE Generally about 1.5 x 1m (5 x 3ft) after three years and then rarely more than about 3 x 3m (10 x 10ft) in gardens, although potentially a tree up to 6 x 4m (20 x 13ft).

Acer japonicum

propagated by grafting.

PRUNING
See Pruning, *Acer ginnala*.

PROBLEMS
Coral spot, decay fungi in wounds, aphids and red spider mites.

ACER Maple

Acer palmatum Japanese maple

" I make absolutely no apology for devoting two pages to this single, exquisite plant. For I am quite sure that in the weeks when the warmth of summer gives way to the cooler winds of autumn, it is varieties of this plant that evoke more drawing in of breath, more murmurs of approval and more sudden stops on garden pathways than any other. Its combination of rich, intense autumn colours and beautiful leaf form (delicately filigree in the most desirable of all types, the 'Dissectum' varieties) is unmatched in any ornamental shrub. But it has its drawbacks. It is jolly expensive because it is very slow growing (most varieties will never remotely approach tree size), not easy to propagate and much in demand; and its site requirements are exacting. But if you can provide it with the right conditions, and can afford it, you will have a garden plant to bring you a lifetime's pleasure. "

Acer palmatum 'Senkaki'

Acer palmatum 'Butterfly'

CARE
Mulch in autumn and in early spring and in addition give a balanced general fertilizer in the spring.

PROPAGATION
Normal species from seed after stratifying in a sandy, soil-based compost over winter but all the desirable named varieties must be propagated by grafting on to the species rootstock; and unfortunately even then, 100 per cent success cannot be guaranteed.

FOLIAGE INTEREST
Deciduous, variously lobed, toothed leaves, in wide range of colours from yellow to purple and usually with intense autumn colours.

NON-FOLIAGE APPEAL
Mature plants may produce clusters of reddish-purple flowers in spring and a few, such as 'Senkaki', have attractively coloured bare winter stems.

SUITABILITY AS HEDGING
None.

SITE AND SOIL Sheltered from cold winds and, in most instances, from very hot strong sun, too. Most soils, but best in deep, fertile loams; tolerant of slight alkalinity but intolerant of clay or tendency to waterlogging.

HARDINESS Very hardy, tolerating at least -20°C (-4°F) provided shelter is given against cold winds.

SIZE Generally up to about 1.5 x 1.5m (5 x 5ft) in gardens although some may slowly reach 3 x 3m (10 x 10ft).

PRUNING
Any dead branches or branch tips should be cut back well into sound wood in late spring or early summer, when coral spot infection is least probable. Also see Pruning, *Acer ginnala*.

PROBLEMS
Coral spot, decay fungi in wounds.

Acer palmatum '**Atropurpureum**'

Acer palmatum '**Dissectum**'

RECOMMENDED VARIETIES

There are approaching 200 named varieties, most with Japanese names and most only available from a very small range of specialist nurseries. I have picked out, therefore, the best among those most likely to be stocked by non-specialist garden centres and other suppliers.

Types with five- to seven-lobed, not finely divided leaves: f. *atropurpureum*, leaves deep purple through spring and summer, turning intense red-scarlet in autumn; 'Aureum', leaves pale butter-yellow, becoming deeper and more golden towards autumn; 'Bloodgood', leaves and young shoots rich blood-red, turning darker through the summer until very dark purple, then vivid red in autumn; 'Shishio', leaves vivid red in spring, then fading to green with reddish tinge, orange-red in autumn.

Types with five- to nine-lobed, finely dissected leaves (var. *dissectum*): 'Dissectum Viride', leaves pale green in spring, darkening slightly during summer and then slowly reddish-green and finally orange-red in autumn; 'Dissectum Atropurpureum', leaves purple, then orange-red in autumn. There are several varieties of this general type of which 'Garnet' is one of the best.

Variegated varieties, leaves seven-lobed, toothed but not finely divided: 'Versicolor', leaves pale green with pink and white splash-like variegation, yellowish in autumn; 'Butterfly', leaves pale cream with white and pinkish streaks and stripes; 'Pink Edge', leaves pale green with white and pink splash marks.

Other types: var. *heptalobum*, leaves seven-lobed, pale to mid-green, turning orange-red in autumn; 'Linearilobum', leaves five- to seven-lobed, deeply divided to the base and finger like, but not filigree, leaves often green and then orange-red in autumn but reddish- and purple-leaved variants exist also; 'Senkaki', leaves five- to seven-lobed, slightly toothed, pinkish-green in spring and early summer, then becoming paler green, orange and finally yellow in autumn.

AMELANCHIER

Amelanchier lamarckii Snowy mespilus, June berry

" On rather more occasions than I care to recall, I have recommended this member of the Rosaceae as the finest blossom tree for a small garden, and so it might be wondered by what token it finds itself in a book on foliage shrubs. Yet that is precisely the versatility of Amelanchier, for it comes closer than almost anything I know to being all things to all gardens and all gardeners. Its blossom is as appealing as its foliage, and while it makes a fine small tree when trained on a single stem, it is equally at ease producing a mass of shoots and having the appearance of a medium-sized bush. "

RECOMMENDED VARIETIES

The normal species is much the best, a form called 'Ballerina' having little to commend it and it must be said that there are also many inferior specimens sold as *Amelanchier canadensis*. Be sure to buy from a reputable nursery and obtain the true *A. lamarckii*.

FOLIAGE INTEREST

Deciduous, small, oval leaves, coppery as they unfold, then green, with orange-red autumn colour.

NON-FOLIAGE APPEAL

Masses of delicate white blossom in spring, a delicate twig form and overall shape and reddish fruits in some seasons (although birds are strongly attracted to them and consequently they may not persist).

SUITABILITY AS HEDGING
None.

SITE AND SOIL Almost any, tolerant of exposure and strong winds, and of both dryness and heavy clay.

HARDINESS Very hardy, tolerating at least -20°C (-4°F).

SIZE Generally up to about 1.5 x 1.5m (5 x 5ft) after three years, 6 x 6m (20 x 20ft) ultimately.

CARE

Mulch in autumn and early spring and give a balanced general fertilizer in spring, at least until well established.

PROPAGATION

By removal of suckers.

PRUNING

Not necessary, but may be pruned to shape in either autumn or spring and will rejuvenate well.

PROBLEMS

None.

Amelanchier lamarckii

ARALIA

Aralia elata 'Aureovariegata'

Aralia elata Angelica tree

❝ *This is a classic example of what garden designers like to call an 'architectural plant'; essentially a euphemism for something that looks like nothing else and, wherever you put it in the garden,* *it will stick out like a sore thumb. It is big in all its proportions, with impressive leaves and an overall appearance that betrays its oriental origin. It will certainly lend a Japanese feel to your garden.* ❞

CARE
Mulch in autumn and early spring. Give a balanced general fertilizer in spring.

PROPAGATION
Normal species by seed after stratifying in a sandy, soil-based compost over winter. Variegated forms do not come true and must be propagated by grafting on to the species rootstock.

PRUNING
Not necessary, but may need tidying up in the spring as it has a tendency to shed its branches.

PROBLEMS
None.

RECOMMENDED VARIETIES
The normal species has greyish-green leaves but the variegated forms are prettier: 'Aureovariegata' has attractive golden variegation on rather broader leaves; 'Variegata' has creamy-white leaf margins and occasional blotches.

FOLIAGE INTEREST
Deciduous, large or very large pinnate leaves, rather like those of a large ash, insignificant autumn colour.

NON-FOLIAGE APPEAL
Masses of very tiny, whitish flowers in big upright inflorescences in late summer.

SUITABILITY AS HEDGING
None.

SITE AND SOIL
Full sun or very light shade, preferably with shelter from strong winds. Most soils but less satisfactory on dry chalky soils.

HARDINESS
Hardy, tolerating -15 to -20°C (5 to -4°F).

SIZE
1 x 1.5m (3 x 5ft) after three years, about 4 x 3m (13 x 10ft) ultimately.

ARCTOSTAPHYLOS

Arctostaphylos uva-ursi Bearberry

" Although those who garden on acid soils have a great range of flowering shrubs of matchless beauty to choose from, there is a rather more limited range of low-growing, ground-covering evergreens and it is on this score that Arctostaphylos *is definitely worth considering. It isn't rare, and indeed grows in appropriate habitats in most cooler parts of the northern hemisphere but, unaccountably, is seen relatively infrequently in nurseries and garden centres. It is important, moreover, to buy several plants if the ground-covering effect is to be achieved quickly. "*

FOLIAGE INTEREST
Evergreen, small, bright green, rather leathery, oval leaves.

NON-FOLIAGE APPEAL
Masses of small, bell-like flowers at the ends of shoots in spring, usually white or pinkish but red in some selected forms.

SUITABILITY AS HEDGING
None.

SITE AND SOIL Full sun, will not thrive in any shade. Acidic soil, intolerant of any lime or tendency to waterlogging although it will grow in relatively dry conditions.

HARDINESS Very hardy, tolerating at least -20°C (-4°F).

SIZE About 50 x 50 cm (20 x 20in) after three years, 50cm x 1m (20in x 3ft) ultimately, although the individual plants run together to form a mat.

CARE
Mulch in autumn and early spring with an acidic mulch such as chopped conifer needles and give a balanced general fertilizer in spring until the plants link to form a ground-covering mat.

PROPAGATION
Most easily by removal of naturally rooted layers but also readily from softwood cuttings in early summer, struck in a soil-less acidic compost.

PRUNING
Not necessary.

PROBLEMS
None.

RECOMMENDED VARIETIES
The normal species is the one that will usually be seen, although sometimes named varieties, mainly of plants selected for more intensely pink or red flower colour, may also be found.

Arctostaphylos uva-ursi

Aronia arbutifolia Red chokeberry

" Another acid-soil plant, this time one very familiar in North America but too infrequently seen in Europe. Although, during the spring and summer, it is the flowers that are the primary appeal, the foliage scores heavily in the autumn, becoming richly coloured, like that of most acid-soil deciduous plants. It isn't, however, a shrub for small gardens, as although individually it doesn't attain a great size, it spreads somewhat invasively by suckering. Its ideal position is on the edge of a small area of natural heathland garden. "

FOLIAGE INTEREST
Deciduous, small elongated-oval, dull green leaves with a hint of red, vivid red-orange in autumn. It needs sun in order to produce appealing autumn colour.

NON-FOLIAGE APPEAL
Small groups of single white or pinkish flowers in late spring, followed by red fruit.

SUITABILITY AS HEDGING
None.

SITE AND SOIL Full sun to moderate shade, in acidic soil. Intolerant of any lime, any tendency to waterlogging or extreme dryness.

HARDINESS Very hardy, tolerating at least -20°C (-4°F).

SIZE About 1 x 1m (3 x3ft) after three years, 2-3m x 2m (6-10 x 6ft) ultimately.

ARTEMISIA

CARE

Mulch in autumn and early spring with an acidic mulch such as chopped conifer needles and give a balanced general or rose fertilizer in spring.

PROPAGATION

By removal of naturally rooted layers or suckers.

PRUNING

Not necessary, but may be cut back in spring in order to reduce size and also to improve shape.

PROBLEMS

None.

RECOMMENDED VARIETIES

You will be fortunate to see more than the normal species, but two variants worth looking out for are 'Brilliant' and the more or less fastigiate 'Erecta', both of which have particularly fine autumn colour. *Aronia melanocarpa* is a similar species but somewhat smaller with black fruit and a soft down beneath the leaves.

Artemisia abrotanum

Artemisia abrotanum Lad's love

" *Artemisia is a big genus in the Compositae with many species that virtually straddle the boundary between true shrubs and woody herbaceous perennials. A. abrotanum comes closer than most to being a real shrub and its above-ground growth may be left from year to year instead of being fully cut back annually. Unlike many members of the family, however, there are no daisy flowers* to *provide appeal but fine, soft feathery foliage instead, although this dies back and browns rather gracelessly in autumn. As part of a mixed planting of contrasting foliage types, it is a very pretty and valuable plant; its foliage also acts as a very effective foil to large-flowered plants placed nearby – I have low-growing, deep red, old-fashioned shrub roses next to mine.* "

CARE

Mulch in autumn and spring. Give a balanced general or rose fertilizer in spring.

PROPAGATION

By softwood cuttings in summer, rooted in a fairly sandy soil-based compost. Also by division in autumn.

PRUNING

Not necessary, but even when grown as a shrub, benefits from having about one-third of the shoots cut back to soil level each autumn or spring.

PROBLEMS

None.

RECOMMENDED VARIETIES

Normal species only is available.

Aronia arbutifolia

ATRIPLEX

Atriplex halimus Salt bush

"It won't come as much of a surprise to know that a plant known as the salt bush is a coastal species. It is a Mediterranean member of the Chenopodiaceae (the spinach and beetroot family) and, like many southern European species, has silvery-green foliage. Like Artemisia, *this is its merit, serving as a foil to other more brightly coloured plants nearby. In mild areas, it is evergreen but is apt to turn yellow (not unattractively) and lose its leaves in colder climates. "*

CARE
Mulch in autumn and in early spring, as well as giving a balanced general fertilizer in spring.

PROPAGATION
Best by softwood cuttings in summer, rooted in a sandy, soil-based compost.

PRUNING
None unless absolutely necessary to remove damaged tissue, as it may lead to dieback.

FOLIAGE INTEREST Semi-evergreen, oval or slightly angular, grey-green leaves with a very fine silvery surface.

NON-FOLIAGE APPEAL None, small yellow flowers in spring are insignificant.

SUITABILITY AS HEDGING None.

SITE AND SOIL Full sun; ideally grown in a coastal situation and may not always thrive far inland. Best in light, well-drained soil, preferably low in organic matter, tolerant of strongly alkaline conditions.

HARDINESS Moderately hardy, tolerating about -10°C (14°F).

SIZE About 1 x 1m (3 x 3ft) after three years, 1.2 x 2m (4 x 6ft) ultimately.

PROBLEMS None.

RECOMMENDED VARIETIES
Normal species only is available.

Atriplex halimus

Aucuba japonica Spotted laurel

"If the opinion of the majority of garden writers was an indication of the value of a garden plant, then Aucuba japonica *would never be planted anywhere. In reality, it is one of the most valuable of all foliage shrubs and, to my reckoning, one of the most valuable garden plants of any sort. Yes, it is commonplace to the extent that it has been grown in western gardens since it was first introduced from the Far East at the end of the eighteenth century. And, certainly, it was popular throughout the Victorian period when it perhaps first became tarred with the brush of boredom that was the hallmark of many a Victorian shrubbery. And it is easy to grow, something that, in itself, is enough to deter many a trendy modernist. But it is also uniquely easy and effective in that most difficult of habitats, dry shade. I have a couple of spotted laurels beneath beech trees in my own garden, a habitat they share with precious little else.* A. japonica *is the foliage shrub for every garden and, with the range of varieties now available, there is no excuse for not growing it. "*

CARE
Mulch in autumn and early spring and give a balanced general fertilizer in spring, at least until well established. It is almost a self-sufficient plant but will be much more lush and effective with a modicum of attention.

AUCUBA

FOLIAGE INTEREST
Evergreen, oval, slightly toothed, bright green leaves.

NON-FOLIAGE APPEAL
Female forms (see below) have attractive, round red fruits (or occasionally, in some forms, yellow or white fruits) in winter if male plants are nearby to pollinate the flowers. The very best berrying forms are not generally the best for leaf variegation so a planting of mixed varieties is the best plan.

SUITABILITY AS HEDGING
Could possibly be used in the shaded parts of a mixed hedge.

SITE AND SOIL
Most, although some of the paler-leaved forms can scorch in hot sun and are best grown in the deep shade that is its special *forte*. Tolerant of extreme dryness and heavy clay, although least successful in very wet soils.

HARDINESS
Very hardy, tolerating at least -20°C (-4°F).

SIZE
1 x 1m (3 x 3ft) after three years, ultimately up to 4 x 3.5m (13 x 12ft).

Aucuba japonica 'Crotonifolia'

PROPAGATION
By softwood cuttings in early summer, or hardwood cuttings in a sheltered corner, preferably in a cold frame, in late autumn or winter.

PRUNING
Not necessary, but will regenerate if cut back to reduce size or improve shape.

PROBLEMS
Normally none, although the shoot tips and young foliage sometimes blacken; I suspect that *Botrytis* may be partially responsible.

RECOMMENDED VARIETIES

The varieties of *Aucuba* tend to be somewhat different from each other in the sense that there is considerable variability even within named clones. The following, however, are fairly reliably uniform but it is important to buy from reputable nurseries. Seedling plants are often available and are much inferior. 'Variegata', female, the form originally introduced from Japan, with irregular cream leaf spotting; 'Gold Dust', female, similar to 'Variegata' but with fewer spots of a golden yellow; 'Crotonifolia', female, large leaves with masses of small, yellow spots and usually some much paler, almost entirely yellow leaves; 'Picturata', male, leaves darker green with irregular yellow blotches; 'Salicifolia', female, highly distinctive with narrow, elongated, all green leaves.

BERBERIS

Berberis (evergreen forms)

If this were a book on flowering shrubs, then the evergreen Berberis *species would take pride of place. As it is, the deciduous forms, by and large, offer more in the way of foliage interest, but the generally unappreciated range in leaf size and shape and degree of thorniness among the evergreens can't go unremarked. For, in a mixed shrub planting, there are no other species offering their particular combinations of characteristics while, unusually for evergreens, some species do, indeed, also offer autumn leaf colour changes. Additionally, berberis have the special distinction of being recommended by the police. For anyone wishing to deter intruders from broaching their garden boundaries, there are few more persuasive features than a massed planting of berberis.*

Berberis x *stenophylla* 'Pink Pearl'

CARE
Mulch in autumn and early spring and give a balanced rose fertilizer in spring.

PROPAGATION
By softwood cuttings in early summer or alternatively by semi-ripe cuttings in early autumn, using a soil-based compost in a cold frame.

PRUNING
Not necessary, but all forms will regenerate if cut back in spring to reduce size or improve shape and with large old plants, it is wise to cut out up to one-third of the oldest shoots each year.

PROBLEMS
None.

FOLIAGE INTEREST
Evergreen, oval to elongated leaves in varying shades of green, some with autumn colour.

NON-FOLIAGE APPEAL
Beautiful spring to early summer flowers in shades of yellow or orange, some double. Most have very dark bluish fruits later in the season.

SUITABILITY AS HEDGING
May be used in fairly informal hedges; taller spiny forms such as *B. julianae* can form a particularly effective barrier.

SITE AND SOIL Most will tolerate full sun but are generally best in light shade, preferably with shelter from cold winds. Most soils but always best on deep, fairly rich loams and much less successful on dry or impoverished sites.

HARDINESS Hardy to very hardy, most tolerating at least -20°C (-4°F) but a few including *B.* x *lologensis* and *B. linearifolia* are more tender.

SIZE Varies with species and variety. Tall forms will reach 1.5 x 1.5m (5 x 5ft) after three years, and 4 x 4m (13 x 13ft) ultimately; medium forms about 2.7 x 2.7m (9 x 9ft) and low-growing forms barely half this.

RECOMMENDED VARIETIES

Berberis julianae, tall, dull green, elongated leaves with some orange-red autumn colours, long triple thorns at each stem node, large pale yellow flowers. *B. gagnepainii* var. *lanceifolia*, tall, similar to *B. julianae* but with leaves shorter and more holly-like; a good plant for an extensive boundary planting as it spreads by suckering. *B. linearifolia* 'Orange King', tall, mid-green, narrowly elongated leaves, silver beneath, few long spines, double, vivid orange flowers. *B. x media* 'Parkjuweel', tall, oval, almost spineless, light green leaves with orange autumn colours, long thorns on stem nodes, yellow flowers. *B. x stenophylla*, tall, almost needle-like, curved olive-green leaves, silvery beneath, up to three fairly long thorns at stem nodes, massed yellow flowers in spring but variants include 'Claret Cascade', red-purple stems, red buds, orange flowers; 'Corallina Compacta', dwarf, coral-pink buds, yellow flowers; 'Crawley Gem', medium height, red flowers; 'Irwinii', low-growing, tiny leaves, arching stems with yellow flowers; 'Pink Pearl', dwarf – low-growing, flowers pink, yellow or bicoloured. *B. darwinii*, medium-tall, leaves small, holly-like, olive-green, silvery beneath, abundant small spines, exquisite vivid orange flowers. *B. candidula*, medium height, leaves elongated, light green, silvery beneath, elongated spines, rather sparse yellow flowers. *B. x lologensis*, medium height, leaves small, holly-like, olive-green, silvery beneath, abundant small spines, orange flowers, similar to *B. darwinii* but not as hardy. *B. buxifolia* 'Nana', low-growing, spreading, leaves oval, pale green, may only be semi-evergreen in colder areas, small, abundant spines, double yellow flowers. *B. panlanensis*, low-growing, elongated, bright green leaves, small spines, golden yellow flowers. *B. verruculosa*, low-growing, spreading, leaves elongated oval, olive-green, silvery beneath, elongated spines, semi-double yellow flowers.

Berberis darwinii

Berberis x lologensis

Berberis julianae

BERBERIS

Berberis (deciduous forms)

" *Although there are fewer important garden species among the deciduous types of* Berberis, *there is one that, in the range of colours of its small, elliptical or rounded leaves, offers an extraordinary amount of interest. This is the prickly oriental species* Berberis thunbergii, *an important ingredient of western gardening* since the end of the nineteenth century. It has the relatively unusual merit, among deciduous shrubs of any type, in providing, I think, equal interest both in its normal summer foliage hues and in its autumn tints. Add to these features its small size and, in many varieties, a very appealing and contrasting flower colour and you have one of the most useful and desirable of all shrubs for the modern garden. I just hope that its familiarity, widespread and inexpensive availability and ease of cultivation don't result in gardening experts turning their backs on it for being too commonplace and insufficient of a challenge. "

OTHER DECIDUOUS SPECIES

Berberis x *ottawensis* is a variable Canadian hybrid between B. *thunbergii* and B. *vulgaris* (itself not, to my mind, a garden-worthy species). It is similar in its reddish-purple leaves to B. *thunbergii* but retains the yellow flowers of its other parent. It is a tall plant, reaching about 3m (10ft) and is best in the form 'Superba' which has rich red autumn colour. B. *aggregata* is a Chinese species with pale green leaves that turn a rich orange-red in autumn. It is a markedly prickly plant, slowly reaching about 3m (10ft) in height with small double or semi-double yellow flowers in spring and the special merit of masses of pale reddish-orange fruits. B. *wilsoniae*, also from China, is similar to B. *aggregata* and also has very attractive fruits but only attains about half the size and makes a pretty, low-growing hedge. It has given rise to many valuable hybrids.

Berberis thunbergii f. *atropurpurea*

Berberis aggregata

Berberis thunbergii 'Rose Glow'

RECOMMENDED VARIETIES

f. *atropurpurea*, red-purple leaves, red-orange in autumn, freely fruiting, probably the best hedging form and will come true from seed; 'Atropurpurea Nana' (also called 'Little Favourite' and 'Crimson Pygmy'), similar to f. *atropurpurea* but more intensely purple and only reaching about 50cm (18in) in height; 'Aurea', pale green to yellowish leaves, deepening to golden yellow in summer and finally rich reddish-orange in autumn; 'Bagatelle', similar to 'Atropurpurea Nana' but if anything, more compact in habit and with slightly redder rather than purple foliage; 'Dart's Red Lady', very dark purple leaves, orange-red autumn colours, rather more vigorous than most in height and spread; 'Erecta', pale green leaves, spectacularly orange-red autumn colour, markedly upright habit; 'Golden Ring', purple leaves that later develop a golden margin, vivid red autumn colours; 'Harlequin', small purple leaves with cream and pink mottling that intensifies during the summer; 'Helmond Pillar', dark red-purple foliage, orange-red autumn colour, tall, upright habit; 'Kobold', pale green leaves, darkening during the summer, orange in autumn, compact dwarf habit; 'Red Chief', elongated purple-red leaves on red stems, orange-red in autumn, attractive winter appearance from the purple stems; 'Red Pillar', purple-red leaves, orange-red autumn colour, markedly upright habit; 'Rose Glow', similar to 'Harlequin' with purple foliage, mottled pink and white, slight reddish-orange autumn colour; 'Silver Beauty', pale green leaves with silver and pink mottling, orange-red autumn colour.

FOLIAGE INTEREST
Deciduous, rounded to elliptical or elongated leaves in shades of green or reddish-purple, some with mottling and most with intense autumn colour.

NON-FOLIAGE APPEAL
Clusters of small, bell-shaped spring flowers, mainly white but usually with pink and reddish tints. Most have rounded reddish fruits later in the season. A few forms have attractively coloured stems.

SUITABILITY AS HEDGING
Several forms may be used for low-growing, prickly and attractive hedges.

SITE AND SOIL Most will tolerate full sun and mottled types will have poorer colours in shade. Very pale-leaved forms may be scorched in full sun, however, and are better in light shade. Tolerates most soils but always best on deep, fairly rich loams and much less successful on dry or impoverished sites.

HARDINESS Hardy, most tolerating at least -15°C (5°F).

SIZE Varies slightly with variety but most will attain about 1 x 1m (3 x 3ft) after three or four years and will eventually reach about 2 x 2m (6 x 6ft).

Berberis thunbergii **'Dart's Red Lady'**

CARE
Mulch in autumn and early spring and give a balanced rose fertilizer in spring.

PROPAGATION
By softwood cuttings in early summer or semi-ripe cuttings in early autumn, using soil-based compost in a cold frame. Some forms (see above) will come true from seed, best sown in a soil-based compost in pans in a cold frame in autumn.

PRUNING
Not necessary, but all forms will regenerate if cut back in spring to improve the shape and, with old plants, it is wise to cut out up to one-third of the oldest shoots each year. When grown as a low-growing hedge, may be cut back lightly in early autumn, clipping the sides fairly hard but not trimming the leading shoots until the desired height is reached.

PROBLEMS
None.

BUPLEURUM

Bupleurum fruticosum

❝ *There are relatively few shrubs in the family Umbelliferae, a family that I am sure most gardeners think of in terms of cow parsley, fennel and countless other feathery foliaged, white- or yellow-flowered herbaceous perennials. And even confronted with a* Bupleurum, *which rather too few gardeners ever are, its family affinities don't strike one as immediately obvious. But*

umbellifer it is, with its tiny yellow flowers and shiny, somewhat glaucous foliage. It is a shrub that has been cultivated outside its Mediterranean home for several hundred years but has never really caught on. And while I can't imagine it winning many prizes, it is, I think, a plant for a mixed shrubbery in relatively mild areas that could be given greater recognition. ❞

FOLIAGE INTEREST
Evergreen, elliptical leaves, glossy and bluish- or greyish-green above, silvery beneath.

NON-FOLIAGE APPEAL
Rounded umbels of tiny green-yellow flowers from mid-summer through to early autumn. Pretty brown seedheads through winter.

SUITABILITY AS HEDGING
May be used for informal screening hedges, especially in mild coastal areas, even where exposed to strong winds.

SITE AND SOIL
Always best grown in full sun, becoming leggy and much less attractive in shade. Always grows most successfully in coastal gardens. Tolerates most soils, but favours well-drained sites in particular.

HARDINESS
Moderately hardy to hardy, tolerating around -15°C (5°F).

SIZE
Will attain about 1.5 x 1.5m (5 x 5ft) after three years, and will slowly reach about 3 x 3m (10 x 10ft).

CARE
Mulch in autumn and early spring and give a balanced rose fertilizer in spring.

PROPAGATION
By softwood cuttings in early summer in soil-based compost in a cold frame. Also fairly readily from seed stratified in a sandy, soil-based compost in pans in a cold frame in autumn.

PRUNING
Not necessary, but may be lightly pruned to shape in spring if desired.

PROBLEMS
None.

RECOMMENDED VARIETIES
The normal species only is available.

Buxus sempervirens Box

❝ *Box is a shrub that is taken for granted and its real merits are rarely appreciated. Yet when you visit as many gardens as I do, you can't fail to realize that this is one of the most valuable, versatile and variable of all foliage shrubs. And a foliage plant it certainly is, with flowers so insignificant that many gardeners who have had box in their gardens for all of their lives would be hard put to describe them. It is, after yew, the second-best species for topiary and is also a valuable hedging plant, with the essential combined merits of small leaves, a very twiggy habit and a tolerable ability to regrow from fairly old wood.* ❞

Bupleurum fruticosum

BUXUS

FOLIAGE INTEREST
Evergreen, small, rounded to more elongated, glossy dark green leaves with some pretty variegated forms, too.

NON-FOLIAGE APPEAL
None.

SUITABILITY AS HEDGING
Excellent, but slow growing.

SITE AND SOIL
Tolerates almost all aspects, including deep shade although the variegated forms are always better in full sun. Tolerates most soils including dry sites but best in good, rich loams.

HARDINESS
Very hardy, tolerating at least -20°C (-4°F).

SIZE
The more vigorous forms will very slowly reach about 5-6 x 5-6m (16-20 x 16-20ft) but will usually be clipped to much less.

Buxus 'Latifolia Maculata'

RECOMMENDED VARIETIES
The normal species is widely available but it is far better, although rather more costly, to choose the named variant that is most appropriate to your particular purpose. The varieties, especially the variegated forms, however, masquerade under a range of different names. 'Angustifolia' (also called 'Longifolia'), leaves dark green and markedly elongated, a rather more vigorous spreading plant; 'Argenteovariegata' (also called 'Argentea'), rounded leaves with white margin; 'Aureovariegata', leaves more or less rounded with golden edges and some golden blotching; 'Elegantissima', leaves rather small and irregularly shaped with white edges, very slow growing and remaining fairly dwarf but with a tendency to revert to green if clipped; 'Latifolia Maculata', leaves very dark green with yellow blotches, slower growing than the normal species; 'Pendula', a more upright habit with very attractive pendulous branches, best grown as a small specimen tree; 'Suffruticosa', a very slow-growing form with small leaves, ideal when clipped for use as dwarf edging to knot gardens and other formal beds but not intrinsically dwarf and will, if neglected, grow fairly tall.

SIMILAR SPECIES
Buxus microphylla is an interesting plant that has never been found in the wild although it is common in oriental gardens. It has smaller leaves than most of the variants of *B. sempervirens* and exists as a number of varieties that differ in leaf shape, growth rate or overall habit.

CARE
Mulch in autumn and early spring and give a balanced general fertilizer in spring, at least until well established.

PROPAGATION
By semi-ripe cuttings in summer in soil-based compost in a cold frame, or hardwood cuttings in autumn.

PRUNING
Box will grow perfectly well without pruning but may be clipped regularly to the desired size and shape. It is a mistake, however, to clip too early in the season as this encourages a mass of soft young growth that is then attacked by the unsightly (although relatively harmless) box aphid. Ideally, it is best clipped at the beginning of mid-summer and then again in mid-autumn.

PROBLEMS
Box aphids, whiteflies, box suckers.

Buxus sempervirens

CALLUNA

Calluna vulgaris Heather

❝ *Anyone who has seen the rolling hillsides of heather in full summer bloom in Scotland or elsewhere will have a mental image of a delicate, almost ethereal purple haze; and probably little else. And certainly, wild heather out of flower is not a compelling sight, albeit a practical ground cover for acid soil. But this is a species that has given rise to a remarkable number of varieties, differing to some degree in flower colour, vigour and growth habit but also, and much more pertinently* for present purposes, in foliage colour. For, yes, it is on the strength of the quite beautiful leaf variations among heathers that they find an entry here. Most have a dual foliage interest in that they change colour through the autumn and into winter. And for anyone with that essential acid soil, they are most important additions to the garden flora. Anyone without acid soil will need to turn, instead, to some of the varieties of the related heather genus, Erica (p.65). ❞

Calluna vulgaris 'Silver Queen'

CARE
Mulch in autumn and early spring, ideally with chopped conifer needles or similar acidic organic matter, and give a balanced rose or general fertilizer in spring. If not clipped regularly, plants will soon become leggy.

PROPAGATION
By short semi-ripe cuttings in early summer in an acidic, preferably peat-based compost in a cold frame.

PRUNING
Trim with shears either immediately after flowering, or better still, in early

FOLIAGE INTEREST
Evergreen, tiny leaves that, *en masse*, give the shoots a feathery appearance and change colour as the season progresses.

NON-FOLIAGE APPEAL
Most have fairly abundant summer flowers in mauves, reds, pinks or white.

SUITABILITY AS HEDGING
None.

SITE AND SOIL
Always best in full sun, although tolerates very light shade. Soil must be acidic, intolerant of any alkalinity and, although tolerant of very high rainfall, it must not be water-logged. Heathers may grow naturally at the edges or on the raised surface of bogs but not actually in them.

HARDINESS
Very hardy, tolerating at least -20°C (-4°F).

SIZE
Differs with variety; the more vigorous forms will grow quickly to about 50cm x 1m (20in x 3ft); the less vigorous to half this spread and barely 10cm (4in) in height.

spring when the benefit of the often attractive dead flowering shoots will have been appreciated through the winter. I find that single-handed shears are much the most useful tool, enabling you to hold the tuft of heather in one hand and cut with the other. Using two-handed shears results in a mass of unsightly clippings that are almost impossible to pick up.

PROBLEMS
Stem dieback and root rotting can occur on old plants, especially in water-logged conditions.

RECOMMENDED VARIETIES

Heather varieties come and go with remarkable speed and, at any one time, over 400 may well be available. I have restricted my selection here to some of those with foliage appeal that have stood the test of time but specialist nurseries will certainly have others that will catch your eye and, of course, new ones appear every season. Nonetheless, this selection gives a good indication of the range of colours that exist. 'Allegro', very dark green leaves, dark red flowers; 'Anthony Davis', greyish-green leaves, white flowers; 'Beoley Gold', vivid yellow leaves, white flowers; 'Blazeaway', yellow-bronze leaves in summer, reddish-bronze in winter, pale purple flowers, a beautiful plant; 'Boskoop', gold-orange leaves in summer, reddish-bronze in winter, pale purple flowers; 'Cuprea', gold leaves in summer, bronze in winter, pale pink flowers; 'Darkness', dark green leaves, vivid red flowers; 'Gold Haze', golden foliage in summer, gold-bronze in winter, white flowers; 'Golden Carpet', golden yellow leaves in summer, reddish-bronze in winter, few pale mauve flowers, very prostrate habit and very valuable on that count; 'Golden Feather', golden, feathery leaves in summer, orange-red in winter, few pale mauve flowers; 'Humpty Dumpty', bright green leaves, few white flowers, a small dumpy bush; 'Mrs Pat', pale leaves with pink-tipped shoots, generally darker reddish in winter, few mauve flowers; 'Mrs Ronald Gray', dark green leaves, purple flowers, prostrate habit; 'Multicolor', leaves varying through the year from yellow, orange and bronze to intense red, few purple flowers, perhaps the variety with the most colours; 'Orange Queen', yellow leaves in spring, gradually turning orange and then orange-bronze in winter, mauve flowers; 'Robert Chapman', golden leaves in spring, changing through orange and bronze to red in winter, purple flowers, makes a vigorous, tall bush, superb; 'Silver Knight', greyish-silver, woolly leaves, pink-mauve flowers; 'Silver Queen', silvery-grey leaves, purple flowers; 'Silver Rose', silver-green leaves, rose-pink flowers; 'Sir John Charrington', yellowish-gold leaves, turning orange with red shoot tips in winter, dark red flowers and a compact bushy habit, arguably the finest foliage variety; 'Sister Anne', woolly grey-green leaves, pink-mauve flowers, low-growing habit; 'Spring Cream', shoot tips cream in spring, white flowers; 'Spring Glow', shoot tips pink in spring, mauve flowers; 'Spring Torch', shoot tips pink-red in spring, mauve flowers, compact habit; 'Sunset', gold yellow leaves in spring, turning orange in summer, reddish-bronze in winter, mauve-pink flowers; 'Wickwar Flame', vivid orange-yellow leaves in summer, vivid red in winter, mauve flowers, one of my own favourites, looks wonderful in winter with coloured-stemmed dogwoods.

Calluna vulgaris **'Robert Chapman'**

CAMELLIA

Camellia

❝ *Camellias have been called the queens of flowering shrubs; although so have a good many other things too. Because of this, their value as foliage plants is generally overlooked but their rich green, elegantly simple leaves have a deep shine that is matched by few others. And a gardening cynic might suggest that the ease with which camellias drop their flower buds at the critical period, just when they are due to open, means that they are better thought of as foliage shrubs in any event.* ❞

FOLIAGE INTEREST
Evergreen, elliptical leaves, glossy and dark green above, greyish-green below.
NON-FOLIAGE APPEAL
Superb flowers in shades of red and pink, also white, verging towards cream or yellowish; single, semi-double or fully double. Some variants also exist with striped or spotted flowers, generally as a result of inherited virus infection.
SUITABILITY AS HEDGING
Only in exceptionally mild areas as components of informal mixed hedges.
SITE AND SOIL Partial shade,
with shelter from cold winds, in acidic, rich, organic soil; any tendency to alkalinity will result in feeble growth and leaf yellowing.
HARDINESS Fairly to
moderately hardy, tolerating -10°C (14°F).
SIZE Up to 1 x 1m (3 x 3ft) after
three years, about 3-4 x 2-3m (10-13 x 6-10ft) eventually.

CARE
Mulch in autumn and early spring with compost rather than animal manure, and preferably with an acidic medium

Camellia 'Donation'

such as chopped conifer needles; and give a balanced rose fertilizer and sequestrene in spring.
PROPAGATION
By semi-ripe cuttings in autumn, preferably in a peat-based compost in a cold frame, or alternatively by leaf-bud cuttings in spring.
PRUNING
None, but cut back any misplaced shoots or branches after flowering in spring to maintain a neat shape.
PROBLEMS
Normally none, although aphids, scale insects and associated sooty moulds can be disfiguring.

RECOMMENDED VARIETIES
There is little difference between most camellia varieties in respect of their foliage appeal but, by general consent, the easiest and most reliable is the deep shell-pink, semi-double-flowered 'Donation'. The only commonly seen foliage variants are the *williamsii* hybrid 'Golden Spangles', with golden leaf spots and blotches and the rare form 'Benten-kagura', a less hardy *Camellia japonica* variety, with golden feather-like leaf markings.

Caragana arborescens Pea tree

❝ Caragana arborescens *is one of the toughest plants that I know, surviving in the coldest and most exposed gardens. I suppose this is only to be expected of a species that originated in Siberia. It is, indeed, a true pea-related shrub, belonging to the family Leguminosae, a relationship betrayed by its pea-like flowers and, under normal circumstances, it wouldn't justify inclusion in a book on foliage plants were it not for one distinct and very pretty variety called 'Lorbergii'.* ❞

CARE
Mulch in autumn and early spring and give a balanced rose fertilizer in spring.
PROPAGATION
By semi-ripe cuttings in late summer in a soil-based compost in a cold frame.

CARYOPTERIS

FOLIAGE INTEREST
Deciduous, light green, feathery foliage, no autumn colour.

NON-FOLIAGE APPEAL
Small, yellow, pea-like flowers carried rather sparsely over the branches in early summer.

SUITABILITY AS HEDGING
None.

SITE AND SOIL
Full sun or light shade, tolerant of exposure. Almost any soil, including fairly dry sites and heavy clays.

HARDINESS
Very hardy, tolerating at least -20°C (-4°F).

SIZE
Up to 2 x 1.5m (6 x 5ft) after about five years, up to about 5 x 2m (16 x 6ft) eventually.

RECOMMENDED VARIETIES
'Lorbergii' differs from the normal species in its extremely narrow, soft, needle-like foliage, giving the plant a feathery appearance.

PRUNING
None; may result in shoot dieback.

PROBLEMS
None.

Caragana arborescens 'Lorbergii'

Caryopteris x clandonensis

❝ Blue-flowered shrubs are always at a premium in temperate gardens, probably because there are relatively few of them. Of the two most familiar examples, the late-summer-flowering, oriental Caryopteris *has the edge for foliage appeal over the American* Ceanothus, *as its leaves are not only pretty but also have the bonus of being pleasantly aromatic. ❞*

FOLIAGE INTEREST
Deciduous, greyish-green, elongated elliptical leaves with pleasing spicy aroma, no autumn colour.

NON-FOLIAGE APPEAL
Masses of small blue flowers in late summer and into autumn.

SUITABILITY AS HEDGING
May be used as a low ornamental flowering hedge in mild areas.

SITE AND SOIL
Full sun, preferably with some shelter from cold winds, and almost any soil, but generally better in at least slightly alkaline conditions.

HARDINESS
Moderately hardy, tolerating -10 to -15°C (14 to 5°F).

SIZE
Attains about 50 x 50cm (18 x 18in) after three years, then slowly reaches about 80 x 80cm (32 x 32in) ultimately.

CARE
Mulch in autumn and in early spring, as well as giving a balanced rose fertilizer in spring.

PROPAGATION
By semi-ripe cuttings in summer in a soil-based compost in a cold frame.

RECOMMENDED VARIETIES
The original hybrid has greyish-green leaves and pale blue flowers but around half a dozen varieties are readily available, differing in flower colour and, in some instances, in foliage too. The following two are the best foliage variants: 'Kew Blue', leaves very silvery, flowers rich sky-blue; 'Worcester Gold', leaves gold, flowers mid-blue.

PRUNING
Cut back hard in spring, either to about 15cm (6in) above soil level or to a slightly taller woody framework.

PROBLEMS
None.

Caryopteris x clandonensis

CERATOSTIGMA

Ceratostigma

❝ *Sometimes called the shrubby plumbagos, to differentiate them from their close relatives, the climbing species of* Plumbago, *ceratostigmas have very different flowers, being fewer, larger and of a stunning electric-blue. They have a special place in my affections for they were the first blue-flowered shrubs that I ever grew but they gain admittance to the present company by virtue of their vivid autumn colours.* ❞

FOLIAGE INTEREST
Deciduous, more or less oval, rather bristly bright green leaves, turning vivid red in autumn.
NON-FOLIAGE APPEAL
Stunningly lovely gentian-blue flowers.
SUITABILITY AS HEDGING
None.
SITE AND SOIL Full sun and almost any soil, tolerating some dryness and heaviness but always best in rich moist loams.
HARDINESS Hardy, tolerating around -15°C (5°F).
SIZE C. *willmottianum* will attain about 1m x 30cm (3ft x 12in) each season after hard pruning, C. *plumbaginoides* about half this height but slowly spreads and, after some years, may become slightly invasive.

CARE
Mulch in autumn and early spring and give a balanced rose fertilizer in spring.
PROPAGATION
By softwood cuttings in early summer in a soil-based compost, or by division. Disturb as little as possible as they take a long time to re-establish.
PRUNING
Cut back hard to soil level in spring.
PROBLEMS
None.

RECOMMENDED VARIETIES
There are two commonly available species, the low-growing *Ceratostigma plumbaginoides* and the rather taller but otherwise similar *C. willmottianum*.

Ceratostigma plumbaginoides

CHOISYA

Choisya ternata Mexican orange blossom

❝Choisya ternata *has been grown in European gardens for around 150 years, partly for the appeal of its white, rather orange-scented flowers but also for the attractiveness of its very rich, glossy foliage. It has never excited me greatly on either count and it has been joined in recent years by a golden-yellow-leaved variant that, I confess, excites me even less but which sells in its thousands and evidently brings about a heightened passion in many of my fellow gardeners, so I must include it.* ❞

Choisya ternata 'Sundance'

FOLIAGE INTEREST
Evergreen, trifoliate leaves, glossy and rather dark green above, pleasantly scented if crushed.

NON-FOLIAGE APPEAL
Small orange-scented, star-like flowers in early summer.

SUITABILITY AS HEDGING
None.

SITE AND SOIL Tolerates both full sun and fairly deep shade but may be damaged by cold winds, especially the yellow-leaved form. Most soils, but least satisfactory on thin chalky types. Often grown successfully in containers, when a soil-based compost such as John Innes No 3 should be used.

HARDINESS Moderately hardy, tolerating -10 to -15°C (14 to 5°F).

SIZE Up to 1 x 1m (3 x 3ft) after three or four years, about double this eventually.

RECOMMENDED VARIETIES
The normal species is the familiar green-leaved plant although there is a variety called 'Aztec Pearl' with rather more divided leaves and with the flower buds prettily tinged pink. The more or less bright yellow-leaved variety with fewer, star-shaped flowers is 'Sundance'.

PRUNING
Cut back the oldest third of the shoots to soil level each year in late spring after flowering.

PROBLEMS
None.

CARE
Mulch in autumn and early spring and give a balanced rose fertilizer in spring.

PROPAGATION
By semi-ripe cuttings in late summer in a soil-based compost in a cold frame.

COLLETIA

Colletia hystrix

❝ *The first time that I saw* Colletia *growing in an English garden, I couldn't believe that anything so viciously spiny and cactus-like could possibly be hardy. But, despite its South American origin, hardy it certainly is in many areas and while few gardeners would call it exactly beautiful, there are many spots in large shrubberies where it could be used to very good effect. But do plant it well back from paths or other places where passers-by might come to grief.* ❞

Colletia paradoxa

FOLIAGE INTEREST
Evergreen, but without any true leaves, instead having branched stems, each ending as a thick tube surmounted by a long spine.

NON-FOLIAGE APPEAL
Masses of small, pitcher-shaped, white, vanilla-scented flowers for long periods in late summer and autumn.

SUITABILITY AS HEDGING
May be used as a low but totally impenetrable boundary if sufficient plants can be obtained.

SITE AND SOIL
Full sun or very light shade in a fairly sheltered spot. Tolerates most soils except very heavy clays, although always best on light but fairly rich soils.

HARDINESS
Moderately hardy, tolerating around -10°C (14°F).

SIZE
Attains around 50 x 70cm (20 x 26in) after three years, up to 1.2 x 2m (4 x 6ft) ultimately.

CARE
Mulch in autumn and in early spring and in addition to this give a balanced general fertilizer in spring.

PROPAGATION
Best by semi-ripe cuttings from short lateral shoots in summer, in a soil-based compost in a propagator with moderate bottom heat.

PRUNING
None; and may be detrimental, leading to die-back.

PROBLEMS
None.

RECOMMENDED VARIETIES
The normal species will be seen most frequently although there is a variety called 'Rosea' with pink-tinged flowers. A closely related species is *Colletia paradoxa* with short, triangular, leaf-like stems on which the spines are borne.

Convolvulus cneorum

❝ *This is a plant that has frustrated me to distraction, for my garden appears to offer just the conditions that it requires and yet it refuses to grow for me. And I confess that there are fellow gardeners who wonder why I should bother trying with a plant that is technically a shrubby perennial bindweed. But take a bindweed's flowers and place them on a bush with foliage closer to true silver than almost anything else in the garden and you will have an indication of the uniquely valuable appearance of this striking plant. It is suitable for growing in mixed and annual borders and on large rock gardens.* ❞

CORDYLINE

FOLIAGE INTEREST
Evergreen, elongated, silvery leaves.
NON-FOLIAGE APPEAL
White or pinkish, bell-shaped, typically bindweed-like flowers in early summer.
SUITABILITY AS HEDGING
None.
SITE AND SOIL Full sun with
shelter from cold winds, and light, well-drained soils, quite intolerant of heavy and wet conditions in which it will sulk then die back.
HARDINESS Moderately hardy,
tolerating around -10°C (14°F).
SIZE Attains around 50 x 50cm
(18 x 18in) after three years, up to 75 x 75cm (30 x 30in) ultimately.

RECOMMENDED VARIETIES
The normal species only is available.

CARE
Mulch lightly in autumn and spring with compost and give a balanced rose fertilizer in spring.
PROPAGATION
May be propagated by semi-ripe cuttings in early summer in a sandy, soil-based compost in a propagator with bottom heat, but a more reliable method is by seed sown in a cold frame in autumn and brought into warmth in early spring.
PRUNING
Very lightly prune out misplaced shoots in spring. Take care not to leave branch stubs as these seem to be infected very readily by decay fungi.
PROBLEMS
None, apart from root-rotting in cold, wet soils.

Cordyline australis Cabbage tree

If you want to create the impression of tropical foliage in a temperate garden with a fairly mild climate, then the New Zealand cabbage tree is the plant for you. A relative of the tender agaves, it could easily pass muster as a palm, and while a yucca will produce a similar effect, no hardy yucca ever grew this tall. But choose its companions with care for, among traditional cottage-garden-style plants, this alien vegetation can look distinctly peculiar.

FOLIAGE INTEREST
Evergreen, narrowly sword-like, fairly dark green leaves.
NON-FOLIAGE APPEAL
Masses of small, scented, white flowers in summer but on well-established plants only.
SUITABILITY AS HEDGING
None.
SITE AND SOIL Full sun with
shelter from cold winds, in light, well-drained soils, intolerant of heavy and wet conditions.
HARDINESS Fairly hardy,
tolerating around -5°C (23°F).
SIZE Attains around 1 x 1m (3 x
3ft) after three years, up to 5 x 4m (16 x 13ft) ultimately in favourable climates.

CARE
Mulch lightly in autumn and spring with compost and give a balanced general fertilizer in spring.
PROPAGATION
From seed, sown in a sandy, soil-based

RECOMMENDED VARIETIES
The normal species is most frequently seen but there are coloured-foliage variants. 'Purpurea', with broader, deep red leaves, is the best known but among others (all tending to be slightly more tender) are 'Torbay Dazzler', with cream leaf variegation, 'Torbay Red', with rich dark red leaves, and 'Albertii', with the leaves striped in red, pink and cream.

Cordyline australis

compost in a propagator with bottom heat, or by suckers carefully removed from the parent plant and potted in a soil-based compost.
PRUNING
None, apart from the removal of browned or dead lower leaves.
PROBLEMS
None.

CORNUS Dogwood

I tend to think of the genus *Cornus* as one of the unsung heroes of the garden. It isn't a name, such as *Rhododendron* or *Camellia*, that instantly conjures up a vision of loveliness to throw gardeners into ecstasies; and yet when one or other of its 45 or so species is seen individually, they can inspire admiration to match the best. And their appeal embraces a wide range of attributes: large and striking bracts around petalless flowers, delicate and arresting overall form (which itself ranges from tall trees to ground-covering sub-shrubs), interestingly coloured bark and, most importantly for present purposes, some truly beautiful foliage effects.

Cornus alba Red-barked dogwood

"It is one of gardening's perversities that a shrub with perhaps the most brightly red-coloured bark of all should be given the epithet 'alba'. But it is the flowers that are white, flowers that most gardeners never see for the plants are routinely pruned back hard to stimulate production of the young coloured stems. The foliage of the normal species is nothing to engender excitement, but nonetheless the species is well worthy of inclusion here because of some of its attractively variegated forms."

CARE
Mulch in autumn and early spring and also give a balanced general fertilizer in spring.

PROPAGATION
Most easily by removal of naturally rooted layers, but artificial layerings or cuttings taken at practically any time of the year will also take root with consummate ease.

PRUNING
None necessary, but it is highly desirable, both to limit the vigour and also to encourage the production of the attractively barked, young stems. Cut back all stems to approximately 15cm (6in) above soil level every year in mid-spring.

PROBLEMS
None.

FOLIAGE INTEREST
Deciduous, more or less oval, fairly dark green leaves, with a number of attractive variegations; some orange-red autumn colour but not worth growing for this alone.

NON-FOLIAGE APPEAL
Red-barked young stems, small white flowers but unlikely to be seen on hard-pruned plants.

SUITABILITY AS HEDGING
None.

SITE
Tolerates both full sun and moderate shade; moderately tolerant of exposure. Most soils, including heavy, wet sites.

HARDINESS
Very hardy, tolerating at least -20°C (-4°F).

SIZE
With annual pruning will attain about 1.5 x 1m (5 x 3ft) each season; unpruned will soon reach 3 x 4m (10 x 13ft).

RECOMMENDED VARIETIES
'Aurea', yellowish-green leaves; 'Elegantissima', irregular silvery-white leaf margins; 'Kesselringii', very dark green-purple leaves, almost black stems; 'Spaethii', yellowish leaf margins; 'Variegata', darker leaves with streaks of white variegation.

Cornus alba 'Spaethii'

Cornus alternifolia Pagoda dogwood

If any one dogwood can satisfy my criteria for a vision of loveliness, it is this one. Despite the Oriental suggestions of its name, this is a North American plant, the 'pagoda' being an allusion to the overall shape. It is, by most people's definitions, a tree, although a fairly slow-growing one, and so I have no excuses for including it here– apart from its sheer beauty, of course.

CARE

Mulch in autumn and early spring and also give a balanced general fertilizer in spring.

FOLIAGE INTEREST
Deciduous, small, oval, pale green leaves, reddish autumn colour.
NON-FOLIAGE APPEAL
Overall pagoda-like shape.
SUITABILITY AS HEDGING
None.
SITE AND SOIL Full sun or very light shade, preferably with shelter from cold winds. Most soils, including fairly wet and fairly dry sites.
HARDINESS Hardy, tolerating around -15°C (5°F).
SIZE Attains about 1m x 75cm (3ft x 30in) after three years, about 4 x 2m (13 x 6ft) ultimately.

RECOMMENDED VARIETIES
The normal species is a pretty enough plant but the best one to choose is 'Argentea', with beautiful silver leaf variegation.

PROPAGATION
By semi-ripe cuttings taken in summer for rooting in a soil-based compost in a cold frame.
PRUNING
None strictly necessary, although any wayward protruding branches that spoil the overall tiered pagoda shape of the dogwood should be pruned out in spring.
PROBLEMS
None.

Cornus alternifolia 'Argentea'

CORNUS Dogwood

Cornus canadensis Creeping dogwood

" This North American species illustrates one extreme of the genus, being a creeping, ground-cover plant, of use rather than great beauty. Nonetheless, so many extravagant claims are made for the vigour and effectiveness of other ground-cover plants that this very adaptable and easy species is well worth considering. "

FOLIAGE INTEREST Semi-evergreen, more or less rounded, mid-green leaves with some reddish autumn colour.
NON-FOLIAGE APPEAL Attractive four-lobed, white, petal-like bracts in summer, surround tiny greenish-purple flowers.
SUITABILITY AS HEDGING None.

SITE AND SOIL Light to moderate shade, on most soils, except very heavy but best on lighter, free-draining sites.
HARDINESS Very hardy, tolerating -20°C (-4°F).
SIZE Attains its full height of 20cm (8in) within one season and spreads by about 1m (3ft) every five years.

Cornus canadensis

CARE
Mulch in autumn and early spring and give a balanced general fertilizer in spring until well established; thereafter, mulching is impracticable but feeding should be continued.
PROPAGATION
By division or removal of natural layers.

PRUNING
None necessary.
PROBLEMS
None.

RECOMMENDED VARIETIES
The normal species only is available.

Cornus controversa Wedding cake tree

" The oriental equivalent of Cornus alternifolia, being of similar shape and appeal, again with a rather special variegated form, but overall more vigorous. Given a large enough area, I think this one has the edge in beauty but it should never be planted unless there is room for its superb shape to develop to the full. "

FOLIAGE INTEREST
Deciduous, small, elongated-oval, pale green leaves, good orange autumn colour.
NON-FOLIAGE APPEAL
Overall shape, upright masses of small white flowers in summer.
SUITABILITY AS HEDGING
None.
SITE AND SOIL Full sun to light shade, preferably with shelter from cold winds. Most soils, including fairly wet and fairly dry sites.
HARDINESS Hardy, tolerating -15 to -20°C (5 to -4°F).
SIZE Attains about 2 x 2m (6 x 6ft) after about four or five years, about 7 x 5m (23 x 16ft) ultimately.

CARE
Mulch in autumn and early spring. Give a balanced general fertilizer in spring.
PROPAGATION
By semi-ripe cuttings taken in summer for rooting in a soil-based compost in a cold frame.

PRUNING

None necessary but any wayward branches that spoil the overall tiered 'wedding cake' shape should be cut out in spring.

PROBLEMS

None.

RECOMMENDED VARIETIES

As with *Cornus alternifolia*, the normal species is a pretty enough plant but a much finer form is 'Variegata' with rather irregular cream-white leaf margins and clusters of white summer flowers.

Cornus controversa

Cornus florida
Eastern flowering dogwood

" This is one of the delights of the New England woodlands of North America and in its coloured-leaf variant, it is equally attractive in old England gardens. Despite the name, its flowers are no better than those of other dogwoods, but with its foliage and soil requirements, it's an ideal companion to rhododendrons and azaleas. "

CARE

Mulch in autumn and early spring and give a balanced rose or general fertilizer in spring.

PROPAGATION

Easiest by removal of natural or artificial layers, but also by softwood cuttings taken in early summer for rooting in a soil-based compost in a propagator with some bottom heat.

PRUNING

None necessary.

PROBLEMS

None.

Cornus florida 'Rainbow'

FOLIAGE INTEREST

Deciduous, medium-sized, more or less oval, reddish-green leaves, good autumn colour.

NON-FOLIAGE APPEAL

White or pink flower bracts in summer.

SUITABILITY AS HEDGING

None.

SITE AND SOIL
Full sun to light shade, and preferably acidic soil, organic, moist but well-drained, intolerant of alkalinity or dryness.

HARDINESS
Hardy, tolerating -15°C (5°F).

SIZE
Attains about 2 x 2m (6 x 6ft) after five years, about 5 x 5m (16 x 16ft) ultimately.

RECOMMENDED VARIETIES

'Rainbow', dark green leaves with irregular yellow-green margins, purple-red in autumn, white bracts; f. *rubra*, reddish young leaves, pink bracts; 'Spring Song', markedly dark red berries.

CORYLUS

Corylus Hazel, Filbert, Cobnut

" There are rather few examples of plants that are so unexciting, if not dismal, in their normal green-leaved form and yet so valuable and arresting in their coloured-leaved variants as those in the genus Corylus. *Admittedly, there is compensation, for nut production is almost always better in the normal species. Most gardeners will be familiar with the overall appearance of the plants although many of the old coppiced hazel woodlands have now been neglected and the plants allowed to grow to full and rather ungainly tree size. The hazel and the cobnut are forms of* C. avellana, *the filbert is* C. maxima, *although to confuse matters, one of the best fruiting filberts is called 'Kentish Cob'. "*

Corylus maxima 'Purpurea'

FOLIAGE INTEREST
Deciduous, large, more or less rounded, mid-green leaves, yellowish in autumn.

NON-FOLIAGE APPEAL
Nuts on some varieties, but pruning for optimum nut production is rather different and good fruiting varieties are better chosen and grown specially for this purpose.

SUITABILITY AS HEDGING
Useful in informal hedges of native plants.

SITE AND SOIL
Full sun to deep shade in almost any soil.

HARDINESS
Very hardy, tolerating at least -20°C (-4°F).

SIZE
Pruned annually, as I have suggested, will attain about 2.5 x 1.5m (8 x 5ft); unpruned, will reach 8 x 5m (25 x 16ft) ultimately.

PRUNING
For foliage production, cut back the oldest third of the shoots to soil level in spring and, in smaller gardens, cut the entire plant back to soil level every four or five years.

PROBLEMS
None.

RECOMMENDED VARIETIES
Corylus avellana 'Aurea' (golden hazel), greenish-yellow leaves in spring, soon turning yellow and then brown-yellow in autumn; *C. a.* 'Heterophylla' (also called *laciniata*) (cut-leaved hazel), deeply lobed rather pale green leaves. *C. maxima* 'Purpurea' (purple-leaved filbert), large, deep purple leaves and purple catkins.

CARE
Mulch in autumn and early spring and give a balanced general fertilizer in spring.

PROPAGATION
Most easily by removal of natural layers or suckers.

Corylus avellana 'Aurea'

COTONEASTER

Cotoneaster (evergreen species)

"Cotoneaster *is not only a very big genus of shrubs with around 70 species from many parts of Europe and Asia, it is also a very important one. I can't think of any garden that wouldn't benefit from at least one or two, chosen from among either the evergreen or deciduous species. Their appeal derives from the brightly coloured fruits, from the foliage, and to some extent, from the blossom but there are few* that wouldn't grace a garden on foliage appeal alone. Despite the wide range of plants included in the genus, I always tend to divide Cotoneaster *into the deciduous and evergreen types and that is the system I have followed here. And again, despite their wide range in size and shape, the evergreen species and varieties fall naturally into a cohesive whole from the standpoint of their foliage interest.*"

Cotoneaster frigidus 'Cornubia'

FOLIAGE INTEREST
Evergreen, mainly dark to greyish-green, elongated leaves, some with late season colour due to persistence of red-coloured dead leaves.

NON-FOLIAGE APPEAL
White spring or early summer blossom, sometimes sparse and sometimes more massed, red or occasionally yellow autumn fruits.

SUITABILITY AS HEDGING
Good with most of the medium-height and taller species which make useful informal hedges.

SITE AND SOIL Full sun to moderate shade, most types are fairly tolerant of wind exposure. Almost all soils but least successful on shallow, dry, chalky types.

HARDINESS Very hardy, tolerating at least -20°C (-4°F).

SIZE Varies between groups. Low-growing types will attain about 50cm x 1m (18in x 3ft) after four or five years and about 50cm x 3m (18in x 10ft) eventually. Medium-height types will reach about 1 x 1.5m (3 x 5ft) after five years and 1.5 x 4m (5 x 13ft) eventually. Tall types will reach 3 x 2.5m (10 x 8ft) after five years and around 7-8 x 5-6m (23-25 x 16-20ft) ultimately.

CARE
Mulch in autumn and early spring and give a balanced general or rose fertilizer in spring.

PROPAGATION
Generally, the easiest and best methods are by semi-ripe cuttings taken in summer or hardwood cuttings taken in winter, struck in a soil-based compost in a cold frame. The lower-growing species can easily be layered and natural layers can usually be found and removed.

PRUNING
None necessary unless grown as hedges, but may be pruned lightly in spring to maintain size and shape.

RECOMMENDED VARIETIES

Low-growing or prostrate types: *Cotoneaster nanshan* (also called *C. adpressus* 'Praecox'), small, more or less rounded, dark green leaves, some reddish autumn colour, white early summer blossom, red-orange autumn fruits. *C. congestus*, rounded dark blue-green leaves, white early summer flowers, red autumn fruits, very dense creeping habit. *C. dammeri*, small, dark green or reddish leaves, white summer flowers, dark red autumn fruits, wide spreading, good ground cover. *C. microphyllus*, tiny, glossy, dark green leaves, sparse white flowers in summer, large red autumn fruits, mound forming. *C. integrifolius* (also called *C. thymifolius*), tiny, elongated dark green leaves, sparse white summer flowers, red autumn fruits. *C. salicifolius* 'Gnom', small, more or less oval greyish-green leaves, white early summer flowers, dark red autumn fruits, forms a compact mound; 'Parkteppich' ('Pink Carpet'), elongated dark green leaves with purple veining, greyish beneath, sparse white early summer flowers, red autumn fruits; 'Repens', broadly elongated grey-green leaves, sparse early summer flowers, red autumn fruits, closely prostrate.

Medium-height types:
Cotoneaster conspicuus (most usually seen as the variety 'Decorus'), small, oval greyish-green leaves, masses of white blossom in spring, small red autumn fruits, spreading, arching habit. *C. salicifolius* 'Pendulus' (also called *C. x watereri* 'Pendulus' or 'Hybridus Pendulus'), medium sized, dark green leaves with purplish veining, white, early summer flowers and red autumn fruits, spreading habit (this variety is also often seen trained as a small weeping standard tree); 'Herbstfeuer' ('Autumn Fire'), narrowly elongated dark green leaves, some red autumn colour, white early blossom, reddish-orange autumn fruits.

Tall-growing types (many of these may be trained as standards on single stems): *Cotoneaster salicifolius* 'Exburyensis', large, broadly elongated, dull green leaves, white summer flowers, yellow autumn fruits; 'Rothschildianus', similar to 'Exburyensis' but with larger, more attractive leaves and richer yellow fruits; 'Floccosus', elongated leaves, white beneath, white summer blossom, red autumn fruits, one of the best shrubs for covering a shaded wall. *C. franchetii*, medium sized, more or less rounded, dark green-grey leaves, sparse white summer flowers, dark red autumn fruits, spreading arching habit. *C. frigidus* 'Cornubia', broad, elongated dark green leaves, masses of white summer blossom, bright red autumn fruits. *C. lacteus* elongated dark green leaves, masses of white summer blossom, dark red autumn fruits. *C. x watereri*, variable, elongated, fairly dark green leaves, white summer flowers, red autumn fruits.

Cotoneaster **'Hybridus Pendulus'**

Cotoneaster salicifolius

COTONEASTER

Cotoneaster (deciduous species)

❝ Among the deciduous cotoneasters are both the best known and probably the least known species in the genus. As with the evergreens, they may be divided into the wide-spreading, low- to medium-growing types, and the taller species but the total number of species is less. The appeal, once again, derives partly from the foliage (with the added attraction of some fine autumn colours) and partly from the late season fruits although the ground-covering and smothering habit of the best known, Cotoneaster horizontalis, means that it can also perform a very useful function in difficult or weed-ridden spots. ❞

Cotoneaster bullatus

FOLIAGE INTEREST
Deciduous, variably shaped, small to medium-sized, variously shaded, green leaves, most with good or very good reddish autumn colour.

NON-FOLIAGE APPEAL
White spring or early summer blossom, sometimes sparse and sometimes more massed, red autumn fruits.

SUITABILITY AS HEDGING
The taller species, C. divaricatus especially, make good, less formal hedges while C. simonsii makes a very attractive, if narrow, informal hedge and is commonly seen grown this way in Europe, although less frequently in Britain.

SITE AND SOIL
Full sun to moderate shade, most types are fairly tolerant of wind exposure. Almost all soils but least successful on shallow, dry chalky types.

HARDINESS
Very hardy, tolerating at least -20°C (-4°F).

SIZE
Varies between groups. Low-growing types will attain about 50cm x 1m (20in x 3ft) after four or five years and about 1 x 3m (3 x 10ft) eventually. Tall types will reach 2 x 2.5m (6 x 8ft) after five years and around 4 x 3.5m (13 x 12ft) ultimately.

CARE
Mulch in autumn and early spring and give a balanced general or rose fertilizer in spring.

PROPAGATION
Generally, the easiest and best methods are by semi-ripe cuttings taken in summer or hardwood cuttings taken in winter, struck in a soil-based compost in a cold frame. The lower-growing species can easily be layered and natural layers can usually be found and removed. A few of the taller species will readily come true from seed, if stratified and left over winter in a sandy compost in a cold frame for germinating in the spring.

PRUNING
None necessary unless grown as hedges but may be pruned lightly in spring to maintain size and shape.

PROBLEMS
Fireblight. Birds often take the berries in the winter.

RECOMMENDED VARIETIES

Low-growing and spreading types: *Cotoneaster horizontalis*, small, more or less rounded, greyish-green leaves, intense red autumn colour, tiny white flowers in early summer, very attractive to bees, red autumn fruits, arching spreading habit with tough wiry branches. There is a pretty variety called 'Variegatus' with paler leaves and a pink and white variegation, often listed under this species but now more accurately as a variant of *C. atropurpureus*.

Taller-growing types:
Cotoneaster bullatus, large, elongated oval, dark green leaves with pronounced wavy surface, reddish-orange autumn colour, masses of white early summer blossom, dark red autumn fruits. *C. distichus*, broadly elongated, glossy dark green leaves, red autumn leaves, sparse white flowers in early summer, oval, red autumn fruits. *C. divaricatus*, more or less oval-shaped, dark green glossy leaves, red-orange autumn colour, sparse summer flowers, dark red autumn fruits. *C. simonsii*, more or less rounded, mid-green leaves, little autumn colour but semi-evergreen in milder areas, small scattered clusters of early summer flowers, red autumn fruits.

Cotoneaster horizontalis 'Variegatus'

Cotoneaster divaricatus

DANAË

Danaë racemosa Alexandrian laurel

❝I think it is the high expectations raised by its impressively classical name that make this plant a bit of a disappointment for many gardeners. In reality, however, it is a sound enough evergreen shrub, if unexpected in its relatedness to Ruscus *in the lily family. But if the thought of lilies leads you to conjure up visions of glorious flowers, forget it;* Danaë *doesn't feature in an account of foliage plants for nothing. ❞*

CARE
Mulch in autumn and early spring. Give a balanced general fertilizer in spring.

PROPAGATION
By division in autumn or early spring, treated in a similar way to a herbaceous perennial.

PRUNING
None necessary but old woody shoots may be cut out to rejuvenate the plant as appropriate; it will regenerate if cut back to soil level in early spring and may be clipped to form a low formal hedge.

PROBLEMS
None.

FOLIAGE INTEREST
Evergreen, no true leaves but glossy green, flattened, leaf-like stems on arching stems.
NON-FOLIAGE APPEAL
Not very much; very small yellowish flowers in early summer may give rise to attractive red berries in mild areas or particularly warm summers.
SUITABILITY AS HEDGING
May be used, as once it was, in much the same way as box to form a dwarf edging to formal beds, especially in mild areas, and very useful for its shade tolerance.
SITE AND SOIL Light to moderate shade; never as successful in full sun. Almost all soils, tolerant of considerable dryness.
HARDINESS Fairly hardy, tolerating around -10°C (-4°F).
SIZE Will attain about 50cm x 1m (20in x 3ft) after five years, around double this eventually.

RECOMMENDED VARIETIES
Normal species only available.

Danaë racemosa

Daphne

❝There are around 50 species of Daphne, *many of them finding garden homes only in the collections of plantsmen, and even there generally chosen for their unseasonal, perfumed flowers rather than anything else. There are two species that I would always grow, nonetheless, for the value of their foliage even if they had no other redeeming features. One is evergreen and one deciduous; and, in reality, both have other attractions too. ❞*

FOLIAGE INTEREST
Evergreen or deciduous, elongated, greyish-green leaves in attractive, rosette-like arrangements.
NON-FOLIAGE APPEAL
Sweetly scented pink flowers in late spring (D. x burkwoodii) or small, sweetly scented yellow flowers in late winter followed by round black fruits (D. laureola).
SUITABILITY AS HEDGING
None.
SITE AND SOIL Best in light or moderate shade; full sun causes little harm but the flower perfume is never as good. Deep, moist, rich, cool, well-drained soil and preferably slightly acidic.
HARDINESS Fairly hardy, tolerating around -10°C (14°F).
SIZE Will attain about 50 x 50cm (20 x 20in) after five years; D. x burkwoodii will double this eventually but D. laureola will barely exceed 1 x 1m (3 x 3ft).

DESFONTAINEA

D. x burkwoodii **'Somerset Gold Edge'**

CARE

Mulch in autumn and early spring, preferably with compost rather than animal manures, and give a balanced rose fertilizer in spring.

PROPAGATION

By semi-ripe cuttings in a humus-enriched, soil-based compost in early summer, although they don't strike easily and it is also worth trying layering which is more reliable although, of course, much slower.

PRUNING

None necessary.

PROBLEMS

May be short-lived, apparently due to degeneration through virus contamination, which may cause leaf mottling.

RECOMMENDED VARIETIES

Daphne x *burkwoodii* 'Somerset Gold Edge', deciduous, the only variegated daphne seen at all frequently, with elongated, narrow, greyish-green leaves with gold margins, yellow autumn colour. *D. laureola*, evergreen, broadly elongated, leathery, dull green leaves in a characteristic rosette pattern.

Desfontainea spinosa

❝ *The Carnival in Rio or the ruins of the Incas may be many people's images of the glory of South America; but for me it is a range of evergreen shrubs that reached Europe during the nineteenth century. Many of* them have the greater part of their appeal in the flowers and so don't find a place here, but one that can readily gain admission by showing its leaves alone is Desfontainea. *It is one plant that makes me long for acid soil.* ❞

FOLIAGE INTEREST

Evergreen, spiny, holly-like, glossy dark green leaves.

NON-FOLIAGE APPEAL

Narrowly tubular, scarlet and yellow flowers in summer that contrast superbly with the foliage.

SUITABILITY AS HEDGING

None.

SITE AND SOIL

Best in light or moderate shade; never as successful in full sun. They do best in a sheltered site. Acidic, deep, moist, well-drained soils, humus-rich and cool, intolerant of heavy, alkaline or waterlogged soils.

HARDINESS

Fairly hardy, tolerating between -5 to -10°C (23 to 14°F).

SIZE

Will attain about 75 x 50cm (30 x 20in) after five years, around 2.5 x 1.5m (8 x 5ft) eventually.

RECOMMENDED VARIETIES

A selected form called 'Harold Comber' is sometimes offered and, although no better in its foliage, it has richly red flowers.

CARE

Mulch in autumn and early spring, ideally with chopped conifer needles or other acidic compost and give a balanced rose fertilizer in spring.

PROPAGATION

Probably easiest by the removal of suckers but also by semi-ripe cuttings in a humus-enriched, soil-based compost in early summer. The normal species will come true from seed sown on the surface of a humus-enriched soil-based compost in spring with some bottom heat.

PRUNING

None necessary.

Desfontainea spinosa

DIERVILLA

Diervilla **Bush honeysuckle**

" The North American diervillas feature pretty low down on any nursery manager's list of popular shrubs, but I can never understand why. The name 'bush honeysuckle' is appropriate for they belong to the same family, Caprifoliaceae, as the familar Lonicera *honeysuckles. And if, indeed, you do want a shrubby honeysuckle for its flowers, be aware that they are considerably more hardy than the non-climbing* Lonicera *species. But I include them here, not for their flowers, but for their very attractive autumn colours. "*

CARE
Mulch in autumn and early spring and give a balanced rose fertilizer in spring.
PROPAGATION
Most readily by removal of suckers but

RECOMMENDED VARIETIES
The commonest form is a hybrid, *Diervilla* x *splendens*, selected mainly for its good yellow flowers but also with probably the best autumn colour; narrowly elongated, mid-green leaves. *D. sessilifolia*, one parent of *D. x splendens*, is the only other common form; long, narrowly elliptical, mid-green leaves with a purplish flush, and small, yellow summer flowers.

also by semi-ripe cuttings taken in summer and rooted in a humus-enriched soil-based compost in a cold frame.

PRUNING
Cut out the oldest third of the shoots to soil level each spring.
PROBLEMS
None.

FOLIAGE INTEREST
Deciduous, rather large, elongated and pointed green leaves, some with reddish-purple tints, good reddish-purple autumn colours.
NON-FOLIAGE APPEAL
Pretty yellow summer flowers in clusters at the ends of shoots. Good suckering habit and useful for stabilizing loose soil.
SUITABILITY AS HEDGING
Not really effective other than for very informal boundary screening.
SITE AND SOIL Full sun to
light or almost moderate shade, in almost all soils.
HARDINESS Very hardy,
tolerating -20°C (-4°F).
SIZE Will attain about 1-2 x
1.5m (3-6 x 5ft) after five years, around double this eventually.

Diervilla sessilifolia

DISANTHUS

Disanthus cercidifolius

Disanthus

  Most gardeners will be familiar with Hamamelis, *the witch hazels, even if their soils and site are not suitable for growing them. Witch hazels don't feature in this book because their greatest appeal lies with their winter flowers. But a* plant that I consider to be the foliage equivalent does: their close relative, Disanthus, *one of the lesser-known glories that Japan has contributed to the autumn garden. I hope this endorsement will bring it a wider audience.* **"**

FOLIAGE INTEREST
Deciduous, medium-sized, more or less rounded, green leaves, superb red autumn colour.

NON-FOLIAGE APPEAL
None, insignificant purple flowers in late summer.

SUITABILITY AS HEDGING
None.

SITE AND SOIL
Light shade with shelter from cold winds, in acidic, moist, well-drained, humus-rich soil.

HARDINESS
Moderately hardy, tolerating -15°C (5°F).

SIZE
Will attain 1 x 1m (3 x 3ft) after five years, about 4 x 2m (13 x 6ft) eventually.

RECOMMENDED VARIETIES
The only species is *Disanthus cercidifolius*.

CARE
Mulch in autumn and early spring with compost and give a balanced rose fertilizer in spring.

PROPAGATION
Difficult although hardwood cuttings in a cold frame in winter may succeed, but propagation achieved most readily by removal of suckers.

PRUNING
None necessary.

PROBLEMS
None.

DORYCNIUM

Dorycnium hirsutum (syn. *Lotus hirsutus*)

" Most shrubby members of the pea family, Leguminosae, achieve their appeal from their easily recognizable flowers, but the southern European Dorycnium *is rather an exception and really does make a good foliage shrub. It shares a silver, woolly foliage appearance with many other Mediterranean plants, an appearance that imbues it with an almost ethereal quality; and it always looks its best in climates and soils that are not too dissimilar from those of its homeland. "*

FOLIAGE INTEREST
Deciduous, semi-evergreen in mild areas, small, silvery leaves.
NON-FOLIAGE APPEAL
Clusters of small, white or pinkish, pea-like flowers in late summer, followed by reddish seed pods.
SUITABILITY AS HEDGING
None.
SITE AND SOIL Full sun, and almost all well-drained soils.
HARDINESS Moderately hardy, tolerating -15°C (5°F).
SIZE Will attain its maximum size of about 75cm x 1m (30in x 3ft) after around four years.

CARE
Mulch in autumn and early spring with compost and give a balanced rose fertilizer in spring.
PROPAGATION
From softwood cuttings taken in early summer and rooted in a gritty soil-based compost in a propagator with

Dorycnium hirsutum

slight bottom heat, taking care to avoid dampness and mould growth on the foliage, or by seed sown in autumn.
PRUNING
None necessary.

PROBLEMS
None.

RECOMMENDED VARIETIES
Normal species only available.

DRIMYS

Drimys winteri Winter's bark

"A plant with no unique appeal in winter and, in reality, named after a Captain Winter but a good, somewhat rhododendron-like evergreen for similar situations. The special attraction comes from the pleasantly scented leaves, flowers and especially the bark, but it is scarcely a species to be used as an individual specimen."

CARE
Mulch in autumn and early spring, ideally with chopped conifer needles or similar acidic compost, and give a balanced rose fertilizer in spring.

FOLIAGE INTEREST
Evergreen, elongated, dull green, scented leaves.

NON-FOLIAGE APPEAL
Small groups of white, perfumed flowers in spring, attractively scented bark.

SUITABILITY AS HEDGING
None.

PROPAGATION
Most readily by layering, or with more difficulty by semi-ripe cuttings in summer, or by seed in autumn.

PRUNING
None necessary.

SITE AND SOIL
Light shade, in acidic, moist, humus-rich, well-drained soil.

HARDINESS
Moderately hardy, tolerating around -10°C (14°F).

SIZE
Around 2 x 2m (6 x 6ft) after five years, 10 x 4m (30 x 13ft) or even more ultimately in favourable climates.

RECOMMENDED VARIETIES
The normal species is the only plant likely to be found.

PROBLEMS
None.

Drimys winteri

ELAEAGNUS

Elaeagnus (deciduous species)

" Elaeagnus *is another of my genera of 'workhorse' shrubs that no gardener can really do without although, paradoxically, with rather few exceptions, might not notice if they weren't there. The only close relatives they have among other garden plants are the deciduous sea buckthorns,* Hippophaë, *and I suppose that the existence of deciduous elaeagnus will come as a surprise to those used to thinking only of the variegated forms of the evergreen* Elaeagnus pungens, *which are dealt with in detail (see opposite). But in reality, this is rather a diverse group of foliage shrubs, widely distributed in North America, Asia and Europe and widely adaptable to the majority of garden situations.* "

FOLIAGE INTEREST
Deciduous, elongated oval leaves, all with at least some silvery appearance above or beneath, little autumn colour.

NON-FOLIAGE APPEAL
Inconspicuous but sweetly scented yellowish flowers in spring, small reddish or golden fruits in autumn.

SUITABILITY AS HEDGING
As informal, tough but not very dense screening.

SITE AND SOIL Full sun to very light shade, in almost all except very chalky soils.

HARDINESS Hardy to very hardy, tolerating -15°C to -20°C (5 to -4°F).

SIZE Will attain about 1 x 1m (3 x 3ft) after four or five years, around 4 x 3m (13 x 10ft) eventually.

RECOMMENDED VARIETIES
Elaeagnus angustifolia (Russian olive), narrowly elongated leaves, silvery-green above and gradually darkening, silvery scales beneath.
E. commutata (silver berry), narrowly elongated leaves, silvery both above and below.
E. multiflora, elongated oval leaves, dark green with silvery flush above, silver with red-brown scales beneath. *E. umbellata*, elongated oval leaves, fresh, bright green above, silvery with brown scales beneath.

CARE
Mulch in autumn and early spring and also give a balanced general fertilizer in spring.

PROPAGATION
By semi-ripe cuttings in late summer, rooted in a soil-based compost in a cold frame; by removal of suckers (*E. commutata*). Most can also be propagated by hardwood cuttings in a cold frame in late autumn.

PRUNING
None necessary, but may be pruned to shape in spring and old shoots may be cut back to soil level to rejuvenate. When grown as hedges, should be trimmed lightly in late spring.

PROBLEMS
None.

Elaeagnus (evergreen species)

❝I know of no other ornamental foliage shrubs that are so obvious in winter and yet so inconspicuous in summer as the variegated forms of the Japanese species, Elaeagnus pungens. *Indeed, few things are as beautiful in the crisp, cold air of the winter's sunshine. But the lack of summer impact is not due to them being masked by grander things, but simply to the colours of the plants themselves fading with the arrival of the bright spring sunshine. They are common enough shrubs, certainly to be found in every garden centre.* Elaeagnus pungens *is not alone, however, for there is a related evergreen hybrid,* E. *x* ebbingei, *almost equally worthy of garden space. ❞*

FOLIAGE INTEREST
Evergreen, elongated oval leaves, most with some gold variegation, especially pronounced in winter.

NON-FOLIAGE APPEAL
Inconspicuous but sweetly scented yellowish flowers in late summer.

SUITABILITY AS HEDGING
As informal, tough and attractive but not very dense screening.

SITE AND SOIL
Full sun to moderate shade, and almost all except very chalky or very dry soils.

HARDINESS
Hardy to very hardy, tolerating -15 to -20°C (5 to -4°F).

SIZE
Will attain about 1 x 1m (3 x 3ft) after four or five years, around 4 x 3m (13 x 10ft) eventually.

RECOMMENDED VARIETIES
Elaeagnus pungens 'Dicksonii', narrowly elongated, dull green leaves with gold edges; 'Frederici', very narrowly elongated, pointed, light green leaves with small cream-white blotches; 'Goldrim', round-oval leaves with gold edges; 'Maculata', the best-known variety with dark green leaves with irregular gold blotches; 'Variegata', elongated oval, mid-green leaves with white-yellow edges. *E. x ebbingei*, elongated oval, grey-green leaves; 'Gilt Edge', broad gold leaf edges; 'Limelight', irregularly shaped gold blotches on leaves.

PRUNING
None necessary, but it is wise to cut out between one-quarter and one-third of the oldest shoots to soil level each spring. When grown as hedges, they should be trimmed lightly towards the end of spring.

PROBLEMS
None.

CARE
Mulch in autumn and early spring and also give a balanced general fertilizer in spring.

PROPAGATION
By semi-ripe cuttings in early summer, rooted in a soil-based compost in a cold frame.

ENKIANTHUS

Enkianthus

❝ One of the lesser-known acid-soil-loving members of the family Ericaceae and included as a foliage shrub with slight hesitation, for I am not sure if I would grow it without its flowers. Nonetheless, it is deciduous and does have rather lovely autumn colours although it is never a plant for the small garden, instead requiring a woodland environment to produce of its best. ❞

CARE

Mulch in autumn and early spring with acidic compost such as chopped conifer needles, and give a balanced general or rose fertilizer in spring.

PROPAGATION

From naturally rooted or artificial layers.

FOLIAGE INTEREST

Deciduous, elongated oval leaves, with good orange-red autumn colour.

NON-FOLIAGE APPEAL

Small bell-like spring flowers in pendent clusters.

SUITABILITY AS HEDGING

None.

SITE AND SOIL
Light to moderate shade, in acidic, moist, humus-rich soil.

HARDINESS
Hardy to very hardy, tolerating -15°C to -20°C (5 to -4°F).

SIZE
Will attain about 1.5 x 1m (5 x 3ft) after five years, around 4 x 3m (13 x 10ft) eventually.

PRUNING

None strictly necessary, but old shoots may be cut back to soil level during

RECOMMENDED VARIETIES

Enkianthus campanulatus, elongated-oval, greyish-green leaves, orange-red autumn colour, pale cream or pinkish flowers; flower variants include f. *albiflorus* and 'Red Bells' with white and red flowers respectively, but no better in leaf. *E. cernuus matsudae* f. *rubens*, elongated oval, greyish-green leaves, intense reddish-orange autumn colour, deep red flowers. *E. chinensis*, large, elongated oval, bright green leaves on reddish stalks, intense reddish-orange autumn colour, yellow flowers with pink markings.

spring in order to encourage vigorous new growth.

PROBLEMS

None.

Enkianthus campanulatus

ERICA

Erica Heaths and Heathers

" *Although* Calluna vulgaris *(p.38) of Scotland and elsewhere is the heather of song and story, myth, legend and tribal custom, it is easily outshone in numbers of forms and horticultural significance by the closely related but much less eulogised genus,* Erica. Erica *embraces over 700 species, of which almost all hail from southern Africa, and there are only a few dozen that are both hardy and readily available enough to be seen in temperate gardens. But among them is a handful of species that eclipse everything else in terms of varieties; a handful that includes those very important foliage plants that fly in the face of the general acidophilia of the Ericaceae and will tolerate chalky soil: the winter-flowering heathers.* "

CARE

Mulch in autumn and early spring, ideally with chopped conifer needles or similar acid organic compost, and give a balanced rose or general fertilizer in spring. If not clipped regularly, most varieties will soon become leggy.

PROPAGATION

By short semi-ripe cuttings in early summer, rooted in an acidic, preferably peat-based compost in a cold frame.

PRUNING

Trim all except the smallest, most compact varieties in spring after flowering. Single-handed shears are much the most useful tool for this purpose, enabling you to hold the tuft of heather with one hand and cut with the other.

PROBLEMS

None.

Erica carnea 'Vivellii'

ERICA

FOLIAGE INTEREST
Evergreen, narrow, often almost needle-like leaves in various shades of green or yellowish-gold, often very pronounced in winter.
NON-FOLIAGE APPEAL
Small but, en masse, extremely pretty and sometimes scented flowers, more or less ground-covering habit.

SUITABILITY AS HEDGING
None, although *E. arborea* will make an informal boundary.
SITE AND SOIL Full sun to light shade, in rich, moist but free-draining soils and, with a few important exceptions, acidic.
HARDINESS Hardy to very hardy, tolerating -15°C (5°F) to less than -20°C (-4°F).

SIZE Varies; most will attain their full size of about 30-50 x 50-75cm (12-20 x 20-30in) within three or four years, but *E. arborea* will attain a size of approximately 1 x 1m (3 x 3ft) after about three years, and will eventually attain about 4-5 x 3-4m (13-16 x 10-13ft), but only if grown in favourable sites.

Erica x darleyensis 'Jack H. Brummage'

Erica vagans 'Cream'

Erica tetralix 'Con Underwood'

ERICA

Erica carnea 'Westwood Yellow'

Erica carnea 'Ann Sparkes'

Erica arborea 'Albert's Gold'

Erica cinerea 'Golden Drop'

Erica tetralix 'Alba Mollis'

ERICA

RECOMMENDED VARIETIES

Just as with *Calluna* varieties, but probably even more so, *Erica* varieties come and go from nurseries and garden centres with great rapidity. The selections that I have made here are all of varieties with attractive foliage that I know from personal experience and, in most instances, they have stood the test of time. Nonetheless, it is always worth keeping an eye open for new and appealing ones as and when they appear. The two principle features to look for are a neat, not unkempt, scrambling habit and a combination of flower and foliage appeal.

Erica arborea (tree heath), short, narrow, greyish-green leaves, crowded on stems, vigorous upright habit, masses of tiny, scented, globular flowers, for acid soils only; 'Albert's Gold', golden-yellow leaves, white flowers; 'Estrella Gold', green-gold leaves, white flowers.

E. carnea (this species masqueraded for a few years as *E. herbacea* but has now returned to its older name) (winter-flowering heather), elongated, narrow, very crowded, variably shaded green leaves, spreading, ground-covering habit, bell-shaped flowers along length of stems from late autumn to spring, tolerant of lime; 'Ann Sparkes', orange and yellow leaves with reddish tips, deep red flowers, a superb variety; 'Aurea', golden-yellow foliage, slightly bronzed in winter, rich pink flowers; 'Foxhollow', vivid golden-yellow foliage, more intense in winter and with reddish tints, very sparse pale pink flowers, arguably the finest heather for foliage effect; 'Vivellii', deep green-bronze leaves, rich dark red flowers, one of the best for flower and foliage combination; 'Westwood Yellow', golden-yellow foliage, slightly deeper coloured in winter, with pink flowers.

E. ciliaris (Dorset heath), elongated, narrow, grey-green leaves, upright growth habit, flowers in threes at stem tips in late autumn, for acid soils only; 'Aurea', yellow-gold leaves, more intense in bright sun, few pink flowers; 'Corfe Castle', green leaves, bronze in winter, salmon-pink flowers, fairly compact habit; 'Stoborough', vivid green leaves, white flowers, vigorous and markedly upright.

E. cinerea (bell heather), elongated, narrow, light to dark, almost purple-green leaves, rather sprawling habit, small, bell-shaped flowers in summer and autumn, for acid soils only; 'Alba Minor', bright green leaves, white flowers, compact habit; 'Foxhollow Mahogany', dark green leaves, brown-red flowers; 'Golden Drop', golden-orange leaves, more reddish in winter, few pinkish flowers; 'Velvet Night', very dark green leaves, dark purple flowers; 'Windlebrooke', yellow leaves, bronze in winter, purple flowers.

E. x *darleyensis*, elongated, light to dark green leaves, sprawling but effective ground-covering habit, tubular flowers borne along the length of the stems in spring, moderately lime-tolerant; 'Furzey', very dark green foliage, rose-pink flowers; 'Jack H. Brummage', golden yellow leaves in summer, orange-bronze in winter, pink flowers.

E. erigena (also called *E. mediterranea*) (Mediterranean heath), elongated oval, light to dark green leaves, carpeting, ground-covering habit, small bell-shaped flowers from winter to spring, for acid soils only; 'Brightness', dark green leaves, tinged orange-bronze in winter, reddish-purple flowers; 'Golden Lady', yellow leaves, few white flowers; 'W. T. Rackcliff', bright green leaves, white flowers.

E. tetralix (cross-leaved heath), elongated, grey-green leaves in cross arrangement along stems, more or less upright habit, small, bell-shaped flowers in groups at stem tips in summer and autumn, for acid soils only; 'Alba Mollis', grey-silver leaves, white flowers; 'Con Underwood', grey-green leaves, red flowers, hummock-forming habit; 'Pink Star', grey-silver leaves, pink flowers.

E. vagans (Cornish heath), elongated, light or dark green leaves, silvery beneath, arching, spreading habit, masses of small, pendent flowers in summer and autumn; 'Cream', vivid green leaves, cream flowers; 'Valerie Proudley', yellow leaves year round, few white flowers.

EUCRYPHIA

Eucryphia

❝ *A well grown* Eucryphia, *in the correct soil and the correct climate, is a superb sight, from both floral and foliage standpoints. On the other hand, a poorly grown one in inappropriate soil is a singularly pathetic thing. They are southern-hemisphere plants, mainly evergreens, admittedly trees rather than shrubs ultimately, but most forms seldom reach tree size in European gardens. Like so many acid-soil-loving shrubs, they look their best in the company of similarly demanding species, preferably placed in a semi-woodland environment.* ❞

Eucryphia x nymansensis

Eucryphia glutinosa

FOLIAGE INTEREST
Evergreen or deciduous with good autumn colours, dull green but surprisingly attractive foliage.

NON-FOLIAGE APPEAL
Superb white flowers in late summer and into autumn.

SUITABILITY AS HEDGING
None.

SITE AND SOIL
Light to moderate shade with shelter from cold winds, in at least slightly acidic, deep, moist, organic soil.

HARDINESS
Moderately hardy, tolerating -10 to -15°C (14 to 5°F).

SIZE
Will attain approximately 2 x 1m (6 x 3ft) after four or five years, then slowly up to about 10 x 4m (30 x 13ft) in the most favourable sites.

CARE
Mulch in autumn and early spring, preferably with an acidic compost, and also give a balanced rose fertilizer during spring.

PROPAGATION
By semi-ripe cuttings in early summer, rooted in a soil-based compost in a cold frame; some species can also be propagated by layering.

PRUNING
None necessary.

PROBLEMS
None.

> **RECOMMENDED VARIETIES**
>
> *Eucryphia cordifolia*, evergreen, heart-shaped, dull green leaves. *E. glutinosa*, deciduous, divided, grey-green leaves with good orange-red autumn colour. *E. x nymansensis* 'Nymansay', evergreen, the most commonly seen form, with dark green, impressively sombre foliage.

EUONYMUS

Euonymus

“I'm sure that I'm not alone in tending to think of Euonymus *in much the same way as* Elaeagnus; *indeed I know of a handful of gardeners who routinely confuse them. They are both easy to grow and very common shrub genera, both include evergreen and deciduous species, both have a wide distribution and finally both have their primary appeal in the foliage, which displays some very lovely colours and variegations. In reality, they aren't closely related but I am fully justified in saying here what I have said previously, that there is a euonymus for almost every garden and our gardens as a whole would certainly be the poorer without them. ”*

Euonymus europaeus 'Red Cascade'

CARE
Mulch in autumn and early spring; give a general or rose fertilizer in spring.

PROPAGATION
By softwood cuttings taken in early summer and rooted in a soil-based compost in a cold frame.

PRUNING
None strictly necessary for the deciduous species, but the evergreens benefit from the removal of misplaced shoots, as well as from a general cutting out of congested branches any time during spring. Evergreens grown as hedges are best clipped twice a year, first around mid-summer and then again early o in autumn.

FOLIAGE INTEREST
Deciduous with elongated oval, mid-green leaves and red autumn colour; or evergreen with small to medium-sized, rounded or oval leaves with very good white or gold variegations.

NON-FOLIAGE APPEAL
Small, yellowish-green flowers in early summer and small pendulous pinkish fruits in autumn (especially deciduous types).

SUITABILITY AS HEDGING
E. japonicus is a good, fairly dense screening hedge, especially useful in coastal areas and often planted around public lavatories.

SITE AND SOIL
Full sun to light or moderate shade, in almost all soils, E. europaeus is best on slightly alkaline sites.

HARDINESS
Moderately hardy to very hardy, tolerating -10 to -20°C (14 to -4°F), the deciduous forms being the most and the variegated evergreens the least hardy.

SIZE
Varies; the deciduous types will attain about 1.5 x 1m (5 x 3ft) after three years and 3-4 x 4-5m (10-13 x 13-16ft) eventually; E. fortunei will reach its maximum height of about 50cm (20in) after three years and spread slowly to about 3m (10ft); E. japonicus will reach about 1 x 1m (3 x 3ft) after three years and about 4 x 3m (13 x 10ft) eventually.

PROBLEMS
Mildew on E. japonicus.

RECOMMENDED VARIETIES

Deciduous types:

Euonymus alatus, elongated oval, light green leaves with intense and beautiful red autumn colour; 'Compactus' is a neater, more compact growing form.

E. europaeus (spindle), narrowly oval, pale greyish-green leaves with attractive reddish autumn colour; 'Red Cascade' has better autumn colour along with better-coloured red fruits.

Evergreen types: *E. fortunei*, small, oval, glossy leaves in a wide range of greens and variegations, low-growing ground-covering habit; 'Emerald Gaiety', rounded, greyish-green leaves with white edges, becoming pinkish in winter; 'Emerald 'n' Gold', oval, greyish-green leaves with gold edges, becoming pinkish in winter; 'Golden Prince', green, yellow-tinged leaves, compact habit; 'Silver Queen', oval, cream leaves that gradually turn green with white edges; 'Sunspot', yellowish leaves with dark green edges, a superb variety; 'Variegatus', small, oval, greyish-green leaves with white edges, becoming pink in cold weather. *E. japonicus*, elongated oval, shiny dark green leaves; 'Aureus', dark green leaves with gold centres; 'Microphyllus Albovariegatus', small, rounded, dark green leaves with silver edges; 'Ovatus Aureus', oval, yellowish-green leaves.

Euonymus fortunei 'Sunspot'

Euonymus fortunei 'Variegatus'

Euonymus fortunei 'Emerald Gaiety'

X FATSHEDERA LIZEI

x *Fatshedera lizei*

"This is a plant that serves as much as anything to remind us that the family Araliaceae encompasses some pretty odd vegetation. For intergeneric hybrids such as x Fatshedera *can only form between closely related genera and this shrub is therefore living proof that the castor oil plant,* Fatsia, *is a close relative of the ivies,* Hedera. *Most gardeners seeing it in a shrubbery for the first time are astonished, as much as anything because it is grown so widely as a house plant and is generally assumed, therefore, to be tender. In reality, however, it is pretty tough and adds interesting and rather unexpected leaf shapes to a mixed planting. "*

FOLIAGE INTEREST
Evergreen, very large, glossy, bright green, five-lobed, hand-shaped leaves.

NON-FOLIAGE APPEAL
Rather inconspicuous green flowers all year, although these seem never to set fruit.

SUITABILITY AS HEDGING
None.

SITE AND SOIL
Light to deep shade; not as successful in full sun, and on almost any soils although best on deep and fairly rich, moist loams.

HARDINESS
Moderately hardy, tolerating -10°C (14°F) although the variegated forms are less hardy.

SIZE
1 x 1.5m (3 x 4ft) after three years, about 1.5 x 5m (5 x 16ft) ultimately.

CARE
Mulch in autumn and early spring and give a balanced general fertilizer in spring.

PROPAGATION
By softwood cuttings in early summer, in a humus-rich, soil-based compost in a cold frame.

RECOMMENDED VARIETIES
The normal green-leaved hybrid is probably all you will find but there some slightly more tender variegated forms, of which the best is 'Variegata'.

x *Fatshedera lizei*

PRUNING
Not necessary, but misshapen branches may be cut hard back in spring.

PROBLEMS
None.

Fatsia japonica
Castor oil plant

"This is a bigger-leaved, more upright and bolder version of x Fatshedera *which must similarly be placed with care. In informal, cottage-style gardens, it will never look at home and it really is a plant to grow in what, for want of something better, I can only call designer gardens of the 'outdoor room' genre, where a touch of the Orient is something to be welcomed. A little bamboo accompaniment wouldn't go amiss. "*

FOLIAGE INTEREST
Evergreen, large to extremely large (up to 50cm (20in) long), glossy, bright green, many-lobed, hand-shaped leaves.

NON-FOLIAGE APPEAL
Masses of greenish-white flowers for much of the year, followed by bunches of black fruits like small grapes in autumn and winter.

SUITABILITY AS HEDGING
None.

SITE AND SOIL
Light to deep shade; not very successful in full sun, and on almost any soil but best on deep, fairly rich, moist loams.

HARDINESS
Moderately hardy, tolerating -10°C (14°F) although the variegated form is much more tender.

SIZE
1 x 1m (3 x 3ft) after three years, about 4 x 4m (13 x 13ft) ultimately.

FEIJOA

CARE
Mulch in autumn and early spring and also give a balanced general fertilizer in spring.

PROPAGATION
Propagation by softwood cuttings in early summer, rooted in a humus-rich, soil-based compost in a cold frame.

PRUNING
Not necessary, but may be cut back hard in spring if necessary and will regenerate successfully.

PROBLEMS
None.

RECOMMENDED VARIETIES
Exactly as with x *Fatshedera*, there is a variegated form, 'Variegata', with white edges and leaf blotches but it, too, is much more tender and is barely hardy except in the most mild areas.

Fatsia japonica

Feijoa sellowiana

Feijoa sellowiana (syn. *Acca sellowiana*) Pineapple guava

❝ *Not many tropical South American fruit plants are likely to be found in temperate gardens but this is an exception, although the fruits themselves are most unlikely to form in cool conditions. It is for its rather unusual foliage that this shrub may be used in sheltered spots.* ❞

RECOMMENDED VARIETIES
The normal species is the only one likely to be found; although named fruiting varieties are occasionally listed by specialist nurseries, these are for growing under protection as in a large conservatory.

CARE
Mulch in autumn and early spring and give a balanced general fertilizer in spring.

PROPAGATION
By softwood cuttings in early summer, rooted in a humus-rich, soil-based compost in a cold frame; also by seed

FOLIAGE INTEREST Oval or rounded, greyish-green with white 'wool' beneath, slight autumn colour.

NON-FOLIAGE APPEAL None unless under protection.

SUITABILITY AS HEDGING None.

SITE AND SOIL Full sun to light shade with protection from wind, in almost any soil but best on deep, fairly rich, moist loams and not usually successful on chalky sites.

HARDINESS Barely hardy, tolerating around -5°C (23°F).

SIZE 1 x 1m (3 x 3ft) after about four years, about 5 x 4m (16 x 13ft) ultimately.

sown in spring in a propagator with bottom heat.

PRUNING
Not necessary.

PROBLEMS
None.

FICUS

Ficus carica **Fig**

❝ *Fresh figs are among the more unexpected delights of my garden in summer; unexpected because the fig is a plant that is so often associated with other exotica such as olives that it is a constant and pleasant surprise to realize that it is so hardy. But it has to be admitted that fruits are really a bonus to its role in my own garden as a very attractive foliage shrub that fills an otherwise rather uninteresting, though sheltered corner. If it does have a drawback, it is that its leaves are so large that they leave a significantly bare gap when they drop in autumn.* ❞

CARE
Require very little attention and if they are to produce a good fruit crop, figs are better planted in a fairly poor soil and fed very little.

PROPAGATION
By softwood cuttings in summer,

RECOMMENDED VARIETIES
As a foliage plant, it doesn't matter which variety you select, but on the assumption that you would hope to obtain at least some fruit, 'Brown Turkey' will prove the most reliable.

rooted in a humus-rich, soil-based compost in a cold frame.

PRUNING
Not necessary when grown as a free-standing shrub although crossing and damaged branches should be cut hard back in spring. When grown fan-trained against a wall, however, cut out any branches growing directly towards or away from the wall in spring and cut back one or two of the oldest branches to the base. Prune alternate side-shoots back to one bud from their bases and tie or re-tie all branches to their support wires to maintain a uniform fan shape.

PROBLEMS
Coral spot.

FOLIAGE INTEREST
Deciduous, large, lobed, mid-green leaves, may give yellow autumn colour but this is not a reliable feature.

NON-FOLIAGE APPEAL
Fruit, if you are fortunate; otherwise, a useful plant to cover an uninteresting wall in summer.

SUITABILITY AS HEDGING
None.

SITE AND SOIL Full sun to light shade, and in almost any soil but the best fruit will be produced on fairly poor, slightly alkaline soils with the root spread artificially restricted.

HARDINESS Moderately hardy, tolerating -10 to -15°C (14 to 5°F) although best with shelter from cold winds.

SIZE Free-standing will attain about 3 x 2-3m (10 x 6-10ft) after three years, about 5 x 5m (16 x 16ft) ultimately. Wall-trained plants should be pruned to within the space available.

Ficus carica

FOTHERGILLA

Fothergilla major

Fothergilla major

" *Fothergillas are indispensable components of any planting of shrubs for impressive autumn leaf colour; with two provisos. Firstly the soil they are grown in must be acidic and secondly the garden must be fairly big, not simply because* Fothergilla *itself grows to a vast size, but because it is one of those shrubs that I find slightly uninteresting, if not exactly boring, for the remainder of the year. It is then much better overshadowed by more cheerful things.* "

CARE
Mulch in autumn and early spring and

RECOMMENDED VARIETIES
The normal species only is generally available although a selection called 'Monticola' has exceptionally good autumn colours, while a related dwarf species, *Fothergilla gardenii*, is a much better plant for small gardens. It grows to approximately 1m (3ft).

also give a balanced general fertilizer in spring.

PROPAGATION
Most reliably by layering.

PRUNING
Not necessary.

PROBLEMS
None.

FOLIAGE INTEREST Medium-sized, rounded-oval, grey-green leaves with red, orange and yellow autumn colour.

NON-FOLIAGE APPEAL Curious, petal-less white flowers in early spring, before leaves open.

SUITABILITY AS HEDGING None.

SITE AND SOIL Full sun to light shade, and in moist, organic, rich and acidic soils; intolerant of dryness and alkalinity.

HARDINESS Very hardy, tolerating at least -20°C (-4°F).

SIZE 1 x 1m (3 x 3ft) after three years, about 4 x 4m (13 x 13ft) ultimately.

FUCHSIA

Fuchsia

❝ Fuchsia *is one of those plant genera that gardeners become so used to thinking of in one restricted garden role that they tend to forget that it has another, quite different part to play. Of course, anyone living in a mild area where fuchsias are naturalized hedgerow shrubs will realize that hardy species do exist. But the majority of gardeners, growing them only as* rather woody summer bedding plants or in hanging baskets, tend to forget this. In reality, however, there are a few Fuchsia species and varieties that are as tough as plenty of other readily accepted garden shrubs. And even more importantly, in the present context, there are forms worth growing for their foliage alone, despite their colourful flowers. ❞

CARE
Mulch in autumn and early spring and also give a balanced rose fertilizer in spring.

PROPAGATION
By softwood cuttings in early summer or semi-ripe cuttings in late summer, in a fairly free-draining, soil-based compost in a covered propagator.

FOLIAGE INTEREST Small, elongated, soft leaves in yellow or variegated patterns.

NON-FOLIAGE APPEAL Familiar pendent, red and purple flowers; although much smaller than those of the bedding fuchsias.

SUITABILITY AS HEDGING The plain green-leaved *F. magellanica* 'Riccartonii' makes a good informal hedge in mild areas and a few plants of the variegated varieties can be dotted among it

SITE AND SOIL Full sun to light shade, and tolerates most soils although best where fairly rich, moist, but free-draining.

HARDINESS Moderately hardy, tolerating -10 to -15°C (14 to 5°F).

SIZE Without pruning, 1 x 1m (3 x 3ft) after three years, about 2 x 1.5m (6 x 5ft) ultimately.

RECOMMENDED VARIETIES
Fuchsia magellanica, narrowly elongated leaves in a range of colours, small, pendulous red and purple flowers; 'Variegata', greyish-green leaves with white edges; 'Versicolor', silver-grey leaves with pinkish-white edges.

PRUNING
In most areas, cut back all shoots to soil level in spring. In mild areas leave unpruned or, if grown as a hedge, clip once in early spring or autumn.

PROBLEMS
Whiteflies, aphids, occasionally rust.

Fuchsia magellanica

GRISELINIA

Griselinia littoralis

" I have never had the opportunity to garden close to the sea and it is whenever I see Griselinia that I realize something of what I have missed. On the face of it, this rather leathery-leaved evergreen species from New Zealand has nothing special to commend it but, in its variegated forms, I find its strong, fresh-looking leaves singularly pleasing. And, of course, for those who do garden by the sea, it is also a most useful boundary or screening plant. "

FOLIAGE INTEREST
Evergreen, medium-sized, broadly oval and slightly wavy bright green leaves.

NON-FOLIAGE APPEAL
None.

SUITABILITY AS HEDGING
Good in mild coastal areas provided not too closely clipped.

SITE AND SOIL Full sun to light shade, tolerant of wind and salt spray, in almost any soil provided it is not very heavy or very alkaline.

HARDINESS Fairly hardy, tolerating -5 to -10°C (23 to 14°F).

SIZE Attains about 2 x 1.5m (6 x 5ft) after four or five years, up to 7-8 x 4-5m (23-25 x 13-16ft) eventually in favourable sites.

CARE
Mulch in autumn and early spring and give a balanced liquid fertilizer in spring.

PROPAGATION
By softwood cuttings in summer,

Griselinia littoralis **'Variegata'**

rooted in a humus-rich, soil-based compost in a cold frame.

PRUNING
Not necessary when grown as a free-standing shrub, although damaged and old branches may be cut out in spring and regeneration will occur from fairly old wood. When the shrub is grown as a hedge, should be clipped lightly in mid-summer.

PROBLEMS
None.

RECOMMENDED VARIETIES
'Dixon's Cream', cream-white leaf blotches; 'Variegata', white leaf variegation but generally thought more tender. Other more or less variegated forms are seen from time to time.

HEBE

Hebe

" Hebe *is a fairly big genus of southern-hemisphere evergreens, often called the shrubby veronicas, and most once belonged to this genus. The majority, it must be admitted, are too tender for cooler gardens for they are prone to winter frost damage. And the majority are also grown principally for their flowers. Nonetheless, there are a few with most attractive foliage also and provided they aren't given pride of place, they are well worth growing. The species I have included here are rather distinct from each other although most aspects of their cultivation are similar.* "

Hebe ochracea 'James Stirling'

CARE

Mulch lightly in both autumn and early spring using compost, and also give a balanced liquid fertilizer in spring.

Hebe pinguifolia 'Pagei'

PROPAGATION

By softwood or semi-ripe cuttings in summer, rooted in a free-draining, soil-based compost in a cold frame.

PRUNING

Not necessary, but taller-growing and broader-leaved types may be lightly clipped in spring to encourage growth.

PROBLEMS

Shoot dieback; root rot in wet soils.

FOLIAGE INTEREST

Evergreen, mainly elongated leaves in various shades of green but also some quite distinct species with cypress-like foliage and shoots.

NON-FOLIAGE APPEAL

Tiny white or purplish spring or summer flowers massed together in elongated racemes.

SUITABILITY AS HEDGING

Taller species can be used as informal hedging in mild areas.

SITE AND SOIL
Full sun, preferably with shelter from cold winds, in almost any soil provided it is well-drained.

HARDINESS
Fairly hardy, tolerating about -10°C (14°F) although this does vary with species and the variegated types are perhaps best not considered reliable below -5°C (23°F).

SIZE
Attains about 2 x 1.5m (6 x 5ft) after four or five years, up to 7-8 x 4-5m (23-25 x 13-16ft) eventually in favourable sites.

RECOMMENDED VARIETIES

Hebe pinguifolia 'Pagei', small, rounded, rather leathery, greyish-green leaves, masses of small white spring flowers, low-growing ground-cover habit. *H. rakaiensis*, elongated oval, bright green leaves, sometimes white spring flowers, a most attractive, markedly dome-shaped habit.
H. x andersonii 'Variegata', small, rounded, greyish-green leaves with white-silver edges, mauve spring flowers, medium-sized, spreading habit. *H. salicifolia* 'Variegata', narrowly elongated, bright green leaves with white edges, white flowers in mid-summer, medium-sized, more or less rounded habit; the true species has the reputation of being hardier than most hebes but this seems less true of the variegated form. *H. ochracea* 'James Stirling', bronze-green, cypress-like shoots with tiny, massed leaves, sometimes small single flowers in summer, low, more or less mounded habit. *H. armstrongii* and *H. cupressoides* are similar.

HEDERA

Hedera Ivy

❝ *It must seem like a stretching of definitions to include ivies in a shrub book, although there can't be any denying that they have foliage. Certainly all species are essentially climbers, scramblers or creepers, adhering to their supports by the adhesive pads on their aerial roots. In reality, there is a group of varieties, based on a form of the common ivy known as* Hedera helix *'Arborescens', that have adopted an upright self-supporting habit on stout stems. These so-called tree ivies, although once popular, are no longer generally available, although well worth collecting if examples can be found. My reason for including ivies, however, is a different one, for I wish to draw attention to their value in creating topiary. By using a pre-formed wire framework and selecting the hardiest, fast-growing, small-leaved varieties, very attractive topiary can be created quickly and simply.* ❞

CARE
Mulch in autumn and early spring and give a balanced general fertilizer in spring.

PROPAGATION
Easiest by layering but also by semi-ripe cuttings in summer, rooted in a humus-rich, soil-based compost in a cold frame.

PRUNING
Trim lightly and carefully, preferably with secateurs or single-handed shears, first in late spring and then again in late summer.

FOLIAGE INTEREST
Evergreen, small, variously shaped, glossy green leaves.

NON-FOLIAGE APPEAL
None.

SUITABILITY AS HEDGING
Can be used in an extension of the topiary principle to cover supports and create a hedge-like effect.

SITE AND SOIL
Full sun to fairly deep shade, likely to be browned by cold winds. For topiary, the better the soil, the better and quicker the result. A deep, rich, moist loam is ideal, therefore, although ivies in general are tolerant of most soils.

HARDINESS
Very hardy, tolerating at least -20°C (-4°F) if sheltered from cold winds.

SIZE
Entirely dependent on pruning and training.

RECOMMENDED VARIETIES
There are numerous varieties of *Hedera helix*; and numerous small-leaved ones suitable for topiary but their choice is usually a matter of availability. Among the best of the commoner types are 'Cristata', 'Ivalace', 'Minima', 'Très Coupé' and 'Sagittifolia'.

Hedera helix **'Ivalace'**

Hedera helix **'Sagittifolia Variegata'**

PROBLEMS
Usually none, but in the close-clipped topiary habit, scale insects, whiteflies and red spider mites may be found.

HELICHRYSUM

Helichrysum

❝ *I'm stretching my definitions again here to include a plant that most gardeners will know as a more or less half-hardy component of hanging baskets and other summer containers. But, in mild areas, and especially close to the sea, the grey foliage of the helichrysums can be a permanent feature of beds and borders too; and it does have a rather special soft and silvery quality that few other shrubs can match.* ❞

FOLIAGE INTEREST
Evergreen, small, variously shaped, markedly silvery leaves.

NON-FOLIAGE APPEAL
H. italicum has yellow flowers and a spicy scent.

SUITABILITY AS HEDGING
None.

SITE AND SOIL
Full sun, in fairly light and free-draining soils, quite intolerant of heavy or wet conditions.

HARDINESS
Barely hardy, tolerating around -5°C (23°F).

SIZE
Will attain maximum size of around 50-75cm (20-30in) within two years.

CARE
Mulch lightly in autumn and early spring with compost but take care not to mound wet and heavy organic matter close to the stems. Give a balanced general or rose fertilizer in spring.

PROPAGATION
By semi-ripe cuttings in early summer in a well-drained, soil-based compost in a propagator with some bottom heat.

Gardeners tend to leave the taking of helichrysum cuttings until too late in the season when I find they are much harder to strike.

PRUNING
Trim lightly in late spring, principally to remove dead shoots and frost damage. In mild areas, will usually regenerate satisfactorily if cut back hard after more severe damage.

PROBLEMS
None.

RECOMMENDED VARIETIES
Helichrysum petiolare (also called *H. petiolatum*), the commonest of the types grown in containers with small, rounded, silvery and woolly leaves on trailing stems; *H. italicum* (curry plant), elongated, narrow, silvery leaves on upright stems, sometimes yellowish autumn colour, clusters of small yellow flowers at tips.

Helichrysum petiolare

HIPPOPHAË

Hippophaë rhamnoides Sea buckthorn

❝ *Anyone who has spent time walking over sand dunes will be familiar with sea buckthorn growing wild. Anyone who hasn't may not have seen it, which proves that as a garden plant it is rather too much of a rarity. Yet it is both attractive and useful; attractive because of its combination of foliage and autumnal berries, and useful because of its extreme tolerance of salt spray and its impenetrable, thorny habit.* ❞

FOLIAGE INTEREST
Deciduous, narrow, greyish-green or almost silvery leaves, yellowish autumn colour.

NON-FOLIAGE APPEAL
Very pretty massed orange berries on female plants in autumn.

SUITABILITY AS HEDGING
Very good as tough boundary hedging, especially in coastal areas.

SITE AND SOIL
Full sun or very light shade, tolerant of strong winds. Light and free-draining soils, intolerant of heavy or wet conditions.

HARDINESS
Moderately hardy, tolerating around -15°C (5°F).

SIZE
Attains about 2 x 2m (6 x 6ft) after five years and about 6 x 6m (20 x 20ft) after 15 years.

CARE
Mulch in autumn and early spring and give a balanced general or rose fertilizer in spring.

PROPAGATION
Difficult from cuttings and most readily grown from seed that is sown in autumn in a gritty, soil-based compost outdoors and then brought into the warmth in spring.

PRUNING
None necessary, but when grown as a hedge, clip once in mid-summer and again in early autumn.

PROBLEMS
None.

RECOMMENDED VARIETIES
As the sexes are on separate plants, it is important to have both males and females in order for berries to be produced. For this reason, always buy certified sexed clones, not simply seedling plants. The clones may not be named, but 'Leikora' is a named female and 'Pollmix' a named male line.

Hippophaë rhamnoides

HYDRANGEA

Hydrangea quercifolia
Oak-leaved hydrangea

" *I think that, if pressed, I might well opt for* Hydrangea *as my favourite genus of flowering shrubs. That is, provided I could exclude the types that every seaside gardener knows and loves – the large pink- or blue-flowered mop-heads – for they give a most distorted image of this beautiful group of predominantly white- or cream-flowered plants. But why,* *you must wonder, is this man arguing about relative floral merits in a book of foliage shrubs? To which the answer is that my favourite of all hydrangeas,* Hydrangea quercifolia, *while indeed having fine blooms, is a unique member of the genus in having superb leaves. Indeed, the foliage is, unexpectedly enough, one of its greatest merits.* "

Hydrangea quercifolia

FOLIAGE INTEREST
Deciduous, very large, lobed, dark green leaves, with rich red autumn colour; although popularly called the oak-leaved hydrangea because of the leaf shape, the leaves are in fact immeasurably larger than those of any oak you are ever likely to see and so the resemblance is tenuous.

NON-FOLIAGE APPEAL
Medium-sized heads of lace-cap-style flowers in late summer.

SUITABILITY AS HEDGING
None.

SITE AND SOIL Light shade, fairly tolerant of wind and salt spray, in rich, moist but well-drained soil, tolerant of moderate acidity and alkalinity.

HARDINESS Moderately hardy, tolerating -10 to -15°C (14 to 5°F).

SIZE About 1 x 1m (3 x 3ft) after four or five years, 3 x 2.5m (10 x 8ft) ultimately.

RECOMMENDED VARIETIES
There are a few named varieties but their supposed merit lies in their double flowers. For foliage and blooms, I much prefer the normal species.

PROPAGATION
By semi-ripe cuttings in late summer, rooted in a humus-rich, soil-based compost in a cold frame.

PRUNING
None necessary, but old or damaged plants may be rejuvenated by cutting back in mid-spring, spreading the work over two seasons.

PROBLEMS
None.

CARE
Mulch once in autumn and again in early spring, and also give a balanced general or rose fertilizer in spring.

ILEX

Ilex Holly

"I can't deny that most hollies are really trees rather than shrubs (and some of them jolly big trees at that), but it is an unexpectedly large genus embracing over 400 species, many of which are tropical, and some of which, strange to say, are deciduous. But within this group there are a few hollies that are undeniably of shrub size and, furthermore, are certainly both easy to grow and distinctly garden-worthy. If they have one disadvantage, it is that when the spiny-leaved evergreen forms drop their leaves piecemeal, they can create an extremely unpleasant experience for anyone hand weeding nearby."

CARE
Mulch in autumn and early spring and give a balanced general or rose fertilizer in spring.

PROPAGATION
Very difficult from cuttings and certainly all but impossible without a misting facility. The selected varieties that I recommend do not come true from seed.

PRUNING
None necessary and does not regenerate well when cut back into old or fairly old wood. When grown as a hedge, should ideally be clipped twice, the first time shortly after mid-summer and the second in early autumn.

PROBLEMS
The larvae of the leaf miner often cause slight disfigurement of the foliage but this will not affect the vigour of the plant and is largely uncontrollable.

FOLIAGE INTEREST
Evergreen, greyish-green or dark green, spiny or spineless leaves with various variegations.

NON-FOLIAGE APPEAL
None on hedgehog holly but small black berries on *I. crenata*.

SUITABILITY AS HEDGING
May be used as low edging to formal beds.

SITE AND SOIL
Full sun to moderate shade; *I. crenata* 'Golden Gem' scorches very severely in full sun. Tolerates most soils provided not very wet or very dry.

HARDINESS
Hardy to very hardy, tolerating -15 to -20°C (5 to -4°F).

SIZE
The varieties of hedgehog holly will attain about 75 x 75cm (30 x 30in) after four or five years and about 2 x 2m (6 x 6ft) ultimately; *I. crenata* about half this.

RECOMMENDED VARIETIES
Ilex aquifolium 'Ferox' (hedgehog holly), small, lobed, twisted and curled dark green leaves with spines on the edges and on both surfaces; 'Ferox Argentea', as 'Ferox' but with silver edges to the leaves; 'Ferox Aurea', as 'Ferox' but with irregular golden variegation. *I. crenata* (box-leaved holly), small, more or less rounded, greyish-green leaves, with very few spines; 'Golden Gem', paler greenish-yellow leaves, most with some variegation; 'Convexa', dark green, very dense leaves; 'Luteovariegata', pale green leaves that have yellow blotches.

Ilex aquifolium 'Ferox Argentea'

ITEA

Itea ilicifolia

❝ *This one of the least known of good garden shrubs and consistently a plant to provoke a puzzled 'And what is that?' from visitors. The most interest certainly comes from the long, catkin-like flowers, but this is a sound, undemanding evergreen for almost any garden that can offer it shelter and not too harsh a winter.* ❞

FOLIAGE INTEREST
Evergreen, broadly oval, somewhat holly-like but not prickly, glossy, dark green leaves.
NON-FOLIAGE APPEAL
Long, delicate, catkin-like racemes of tiny greenish-white flowers in late summer.
SUITABILITY AS HEDGING
None.
SITE AND SOIL Full sun to
moderate shade with some shelter from cold winds; tolerates most soil types.
HARDINESS Moderately hardy,
tolerating around -15°C (5°F).
SIZE Will attain about 1 x 1m
(3 x 3ft) after four or five years, about 4 x 3m (13 x 10ft) ultimately in mild areas.

RECOMMENDED VARIETIES
Normal species only available.

CARE
Mulch twice, once in autumn and again in early spring, and also give a balanced general or rose fertilizer in spring.
PROPAGATION
Propagation best by semi-ripe cuttings

Itea ilicifolia

taken in summer and rooted in a humus-rich, soil-based compost in a cold frame.
PRUNING
None necessary.
PROBLEMS
None.

Laurus nobilis
Sweet bay,
Bay laurel

❝ *I still have to think twice to remind myself which laurel is which. For ironically, the true laurel is a* Prunus, *whereas* Laurus nobilis *is the bay, much beloved of cooks and of smart city florists who sell potted, neatly clipped standard plants at prices to make your toes curl. It is a good evergreen, especially for the more formal garden. Although it has the habit of being browned or killed back in hard winters, it is robust and vigorous enough to shoot again from very old wood.* ❞

FOLIAGE INTEREST
Evergreen, narrowly elongated, medium-sized, dark green leaves.
NON-FOLIAGE APPEAL
Yellowish-green flowers in early summer.
SUITABILITY AS HEDGING
Makes a good, fairly dense hedge but only really useful in milder areas where there is no likelihood of winter die-back.
SITE AND SOIL Full sun to
fairly deep shade but must have shelter from cold winds. Tolerates most soils provided not very heavy and wet.
HARDINESS Moderately hardy,
tolerating -10 to -15°C (14 to 5°F).
SIZE About 1.5 x 1.5m (5 x 5ft)
after five years; unpruned, will eventually attain tree size of about 12 x 9m (40 x 30ft).

Laurus nobilis

CARE
Mulch in autumn and early spring and also give a balanced general fertilizer in spring.

LAVANDULA

PROPAGATION
By semi-ripe cuttings in late summer rooted in a humus-rich, soil-based compost in a cold frame.

PRUNING
None strictly necessary, but plants may be clipped to shape once in late spring and again in late summer. Old or damaged plants may be rejuvenated by cutting back hard into old wood in mid-spring.

PROBLEMS
Scale insects, leading to the development of sooty mould.

RECOMMENDED VARIETIES
The normal species is the one most frequently seen, but there is a more or less yellow-leaved form called 'Aurea' which is not a true enough yellow to be really appealing and always seems to look rather unhealthy.

Lavandula stoechas

Lavandula Lavender

"It's almost impossible to conjure up an image of lavenders without thinking of perfume, pot-pourri and, of course, the flowers from which both come. Though lavender is in fact in flower for a relatively short time, I have some lengths of low lavender edging that confer a singularly attractive appearance to the more formal parts of my garden at all times of year. And they do it by being effective foliage shrubs, a role that is too often overlooked, as well as by producing pleasantly perfumed summer flowers. "

FOLIAGE INTEREST
Evergreen, very narrow, elongated, silvery-green leaves, more or less closely borne on upright shoots.

NON-FOLIAGE APPEAL
Small purple, white or lavender-coloured flowers in neat cylindrical heads; perfume in many varieties.

SUITABILITY AS HEDGING
Appropriate varieties make good, low-growing, neat edging.

SITE AND SOIL
Full sun, best in light, moderately rich and free-draining soils but will tolerate most soils except very heavy and wet sites.

HARDINESS
Very hardy, tolerating -20°C (-4°F).

SIZE
Without clipping, dwarf varieties will attain approximately 60 x 60cm (24 x 24in) after four years; the taller types about 1 x 1m (3 x 3ft) eventually.

CARE
Mulch in autumn and early spring and give a balanced rose fertilizer in spring.

PROPAGATION
Propagate by semi-ripe cuttings taken in late summer, rooted in a reasonably well-drained, soil-based compost in a cold frame.

RECOMMENDED VARIETIES
As foliage plants, lavenders may be divided into the lower-growing varieties, most suitable for dwarf hedging, and the taller forms, best grown as isolated specimens. Both have similar leaves.
Lavandula angustifolia (old English lavender), among the best low-growing forms are 'Hidcote', purple-blue flowers; 'Munstead', lavender-blue flowers; 'Nana Alba', white flowers; and 'Twickel Purple', purple flowers, rather more wide-spreading. Among the best taller types are 'Loddon Pink', with pink flowers, and related hybrids such as 'Grappenhall', with lavender flowers.
L. stoechas (French lavender), purple flowers of rather peculiar form with petals emerging from the tips of small, cylindrical heads.

PRUNING
None necessary, but plants are best clipped fairly hard just after the flowers have faded. Clip just into the woody growth at the base of the flowers. Old and misshapen plants will regenerate if cut back into fairly old wood.

PROBLEMS
None.

LEUCOTHOË

Leucothoë fontanesiana

" *This is a shrub that has consistently failed to perform for me, a circumstance that I blame on my garden and my insistence on trying to grow things for which my soil is unsuited, rather than on the poor plant itself. Even in ideal conditions it will never be stunning, but it does make a very good species for underplanting more exciting things in moist, acidic and slightly shady places.* "

FOLIAGE INTEREST
Evergreen, broadly elongated, pointed, light green leaves.
NON-FOLIAGE APPEAL
Dangling white flowers in early summer.
SUITABILITY AS HEDGING
None.
SITE AND SOIL Light to moderate or almost deep shade, in acidic, moist, humus-rich soil, very intolerant of dryness.
HARDINESS Very hardy, tolerating -20°C (-4°F).
SIZE About 1 x 1m (3 x 3ft) after four or five years, double this eventually.

CARE
Mulch in autumn and early spring, ideally with chopped conifer needles or similar acidic material, and give a balanced general fertilizer in spring.
PROPAGATION
By layering, also softwood cuttings in early summer rooted in an acidic, organic compost in a covered frame.

Leucothoë fontanesiana **'Rainbow'**

PRUNING
None necessary, but plants will generally look best if up to one-third of the shoots are cut back to soil level each spring, although this may be difficult to achieve if the plant is grown in a dense, crowded shrubbery.
PROBLEMS
None.

RECOMMENDED VARIETIES
'Rainbow', pink and yellow leaf variegation.

Ligustrum Privet

" *There are many gardeners, and I am one of them, who would like to see fewer evergreen privet hedges. But the Oriental privets are Jekyll and Hyde plants, for within the 'green hedging' species,* Ligustrum ovalifolium, *are to be found one good and one very good foliage variant; and within the genus, there are a number of other appealing species that are too often hidden beneath the blanket of distaste that has come to surround the group.* "

RECOMMENDED VARIETIES
Ligustrum ovalifolium 'Aureum', clear golden leaves; 'Argenteum', grey-green leaves with irregular white edges. *L. lucidum* 'Excelsum Superbum', yellow and cream leaf edges; 'Tricolor' cream-white leaf variegation with pinkish edges. *L.* 'Vicaryi', pale green to yellow leaves. *L. japonicum* 'Rotundifolium', rounded, glossy, leathery dark green leaves on a dwarf, slow-growing plant.

Ligustrum ovalifolium **'Aureum'**

LIGUSTRUM

FOLIAGE INTEREST
Evergreen, more or less broadly elongated leaves, variously coloured or variegated (except *L. japonicum*, see left).

NON-FOLIAGE APPEAL
Masses of whitish, spicy-scented flowers in summer.

SUITABILITY AS HEDGING
All taller forms make effective, fairly dense hedges but *L. ovalifolium* 'Aureum' is the best.

SITE AND SOIL
Full sun to fairly deep shade. Tolerates most soils but least reliable on very dry or very wet sites.

HARDINESS
Very hardy, tolerating at least -20°C (-4°F).

SIZE
Without clipping, taller forms will attain about 2 x 1.5m (6 x 5ft) after five years and 5-7 x 3-5m (16-23 x 10-16ft) eventually; *L. lucidum* will eventually reach about 10 x 5m (30 x 16ft) while *L. japonicum* 'Rotundifolium' will barely exceed 1 x 1m (3 x 3ft).

CARE
Mulch in autumn and early spring; give a balanced general fertilizer in spring.

PROPAGATION
By semi-ripe cuttings in summer rooted in a soil-based compost in a cold frame, or by hardwood cuttings rooted in a soil-based compost in a covered cold frame in winter.

PRUNING
None for *Ligustrum japonicum* but clip other forms in spring to encourage fresh new growth. Taller forms grown as hedges should be clipped two or three times from spring to autumn.

PROBLEMS
Aphids.

Lippia citriodora

Lippia citriodora Lemon verbena

❝ *Barely a shrub and simply a herb by many people's reckoning, the lemon verbena, even if grown as a short-term prospect, is a valuable plant quite apart from its role in the herb garden. This is because of its dainty and beautifully perfumed foliage. The most attractive way that I have ever seen it grown was on a warm wall overlooking a small formal garden where it had been fan-trained. The reflected heat brought out the perfume exquisitely.* ❞

FOLIAGE INTEREST
Deciduous, elongated, grey-green leaves with strong lemon perfume when crushed or exposed to sun.

NON-FOLIAGE APPEAL
Sprays of delicate lavender-coloured flowers in summer.

SUITABILITY AS HEDGING
None.

SITE AND SOIL
Full sun, in light, free-draining, preferably not very rich soils.

HARDINESS
Moderately hardy, tolerating -10°C (14°F).

SIZE
New shoots attain maximum size of approximately 1 x 1m (3 x 3ft) within about the first year.

CARE
Mulch in autumn and early spring; give a balanced general fertilizer in spring.

PROPAGATION
By semi-ripe cuttings in late summer, rooted in a free-draining, soil-based compost in a cold frame.

PRUNING
Most effective when cut back to soil level each spring but, if wall-trained as I have described, it is necessary to take out about one-third of the shoots selectively each year.

PROBLEMS
None.

RECOMMENDED VARIETIES
Normal species only available, sometimes now called *Aloysia triphylla*.

LOMATIA

Lomatia ferruginea

❝ *This is a South American shrub that looks and is fairly tender, but that is no reason for its relative rarity even in mild and otherwise suitable gardens. The large, much-divided leaves are perhaps more reminiscent of palm fronds than anything else, the ultimate segments being almost grassy in appearance. It is particularly valuable in giving an exotic and tropical feel to a garden on an acidic soil; and that alone is a special enough feature, for there are few acid-soil shrubs with quite this individual character.* ❞

FOLIAGE INTEREST
Evergreen, unusually shaped, palm-like, light green leaves.
NON-FOLIAGE APPEAL
Masses of small, reddish flowers in summer.
SUITABILITY AS HEDGING
None.
SITE AND SOIL Full sun to light shade, in acidic, but preferably fairly free-draining soil; acidic sandy soils are ideal.
HARDINESS Fairly hardy, tolerating -5 to -10°C (23 to 14°F).
SIZE Will attain about 2 x 2m (6 x 6ft) in four or five years, up to three times this eventually in mild areas.

CARE
Mulch in autumn and early spring and give a balanced general or rose fertilizer in spring.

Lomatia ferruginea

RECOMMENDED VARIETIES
Normal species only available.

PROPAGATION
By semi-ripe cuttings in summer, rooted in a free-draining and preferably acidic compost in a covered cold frame.
PRUNING
None necessary, but remove two or three oldest shoots each year in spring.
PROBLEMS
None.

Lonicera nitida

❝ *Even the many gardeners familiar with this now rather common shrub will not associate it with the honeysuckles, to which it is closely related. Yet Lonicera is one of the most diverse of all genera of hardy woody plants, embracing both climbers and shrubs, widely ranging in vigour, and of both deciduous and evergreen habits. I have detailed the climbers in* Best Climbers, Book 1 *of this series, and although there are other foliage shrubs in the genus,* Lonicera nitida *is easily the most versatile among them.* ❞

FOLIAGE INTEREST
Evergreen, small, rounded, yellow leaves.
NON-FOLIAGE APPEAL
None.
SUITABILITY AS HEDGING
Very good as a fairly dense, brightly coloured hedge of medium height.
SITE AND SOIL Full sun to moderate shade, in most soils except very dry or very wet sites.
HARDINESS Hardy, tolerating about -15°C (5°F).
SIZE Will attain about 1 x 1.5m (3 x 5ft) in four or five years, up to 2 x 2m (6 x 6ft) eventually.

RECOMMENDED VARIETIES
'Baggesen's Gold' is the best and most readily available form.

CARE
Mulch in autumn and early spring and give a balanced general or rose fertilizer in spring.
PROPAGATION
By semi-ripe cuttings in summer, rooted in a soil-based compost in a cold frame, or by hardwood cuttings in a covered cold frame in winter.
PRUNING
Cut out up to one-third of the oldest

MAGNOLIA

Lonicera nitida **'Baggesen's Gold'**

shoots each year in spring. If grown as a hedge, clip two or three times from mid-spring until mid-autumn.

PROBLEMS

None.

Magnolia grandiflora

" *Grandiflora it may be, but it is as a grand evergreen that this superb North American plant finds itself on these pages. Furthermore, it is almost the only really hardy evergreen magnolia. Yes, I realize that, in the fullness of time, it will become a tree, but until it does so, there will be over 15 or more years when you can pretend that it is a shrub. And with leaves like nothing else, I think you are entitled to think of the present only.* "

CARE

Mulch in autumn and early spring and give a balanced rose fertilizer in spring.

PROPAGATION

The species will come true from seed when sown fresh in a gritty, soil-based

Magnolia grandiflora

compost in autumn and left to stratify over winter. Selected forms may be raised from semi-ripe cuttings taken in summer and rooted in a soil-based compost in a cold frame, but they are more reliably propagated by grafting on to the species rootstock.

PRUNING

None necessary, but as the wood is fairly brittle, it is commonly damaged in the winter and broken branches should then be cut back to the junction with the next major shoot.

PROBLEMS

None.

FOLIAGE INTEREST

Evergreen, large or very large, elongated oval, glossy, dark green leaves with brown felt-like indumentum beneath.

NON-FOLIAGE APPEAL

Huge, white, saucer-like flowers produced over a long period from late summer onwards.

SUITABILITY AS HEDGING

None.

SITE AND SOIL Full sun to moderate shade with shelter from cold winds but, contrary to what is often imagined, it is not exclusively a wall shrub. Tolerates most soils but least reliable on very dry and alkaline sites although, as with other magnolias, the often stated requirement for acidic soils is a myth.

HARDINESS Very hardy, tolerating -20°C (-4°F) provided there is shelter from strong winds although it should be borne in mind that heavy snow falls may break branches.

SIZE Will attain about 3 x 2m (10 x 6ft) after five years and at least 8 x 5m (25 x 16ft) eventually in favourable sites.

RECOMMENDED VARIETIES

The normal species is probably as good as any for foliage appeal and some of the hardier forms selected for flowering at an early age, such as 'Goliath', have less of the appealing brown 'felt', known as indumentum, beneath the leaves. Perhaps the loveliest leaves of all are on 'Ferruginea', but this is barely hardy.

MAHONIA

Mahonia

"In popular gardening, for many years the name mahonia meant simply the Oregon grape, Mahonia aquifolium, *a good enough plant, and in its purple-leaved variant rather an attractive foliage shrub. But recently, some of the rather less hardy but much lovelier hybrids known collectively as* Mahonia x media *have become much more widely available, and their combination of floral and foliar appeal makes them compelling plants for slightly sheltered spots.* **"**

FOLIAGE INTEREST Leaflets divided into leaves with prickles, purple in M. aquifolium 'Atropurpurea', large and dull green in the hybrids.

NON-FOLIAGE APPEAL Compact racemes of massed yellow flowers early in the spring (M. aquifolium) or much longer and weeping in late autumn and winter (M. x media 'Charity' and its relatives).

SUITABILITY AS HEDGING Normally none although M. aquifolium can be used to make a low prickly screen.

SITE AND SOIL Full sun to light shade (hybrids) or deep shade (M. aquifolium). Tolerates most soils but not reliable on very dry sites and will perform much better in deep rich loam.

HARDINESS Very hardy (M. aquifolium) tolerating -20°C (-4°F); moderately hardy (others), tolerating -15°C (5°F).

SIZE M. aquifolium will attain its maximum height of about 1-1.5m (3-5ft) after four years, and then creeps slowly outwards to reach 3m (10ft). M. x media 'Charity' will attain about 2-3 x 3m (6-10 x 10ft) after five years and 5 x 4m (16 x 13ft) eventually.

Mahonia x media 'Charity'

Mahonia aquifolium 'Atropurpurea'

RECOMMENDED VARIETIES
The best foliar form of *Mahonia aquifolium* is 'Atropurpurea'. The best and hardiest of the hybrids is M. x *media* 'Charity'.

MYRTUS

CARE
Mulch in autumn and early spring and give a balanced rose fertilizer in spring.

PROPAGATION
Mahonias are notoriously difficult to strike from cuttings and much the best plan is to layer them or, if you are fortunate, to remove already rooted side-shoots.

PRUNING
None necessary on M. aquifolium but the oldest shoots should be cut back to soil level every two or three years. On the hybrids, a more compact plant can be obtained by cutting back the non-flowered shoots by about half in mid-spring.

PROBLEMS
Rust may occasionally be troublesome, especially on M. aquifolium.

Myrtus communis Myrtle

> " I was taken to task a short while ago for stating that my garden was not mild enough for me to grow myrtle. Gardeners from colder areas said they had succeeded. So I am giving it another try: perhaps it is a plant that I have always thought to be more tender than it actually is. And if so, I am delighted, for it is an evocatively lovely evergreen with delicious perfume emanating from the foliage, especially when the leaves are crushed. "

CARE
Mulch in autumn and early spring and give a balanced rose fertilizer in spring.

FOLIAGE INTEREST
Evergreen, small, rounded, dark green leaves.

NON-FOLIAGE APPEAL
Masses of small, dainty, feathery flowers in summer, followed by black-purple berries in autumn.

SUITABILITY AS HEDGING
None, other than in truly mild areas where it is reliable in the open, away from shelter, when it will form a neat, compact low boundary.

SITE AND SOIL Full sun to moderate shade with shelter from cold winds. Tolerates most soils but not reliable on wet and cold sites.

HARDINESS Fairly to moderately hardy, tolerating about -10°C (14°F).

SIZE Will attain a size of about 1 x 1m (3 x 3ft) in five years, and approximately 5 x 3m (16 x 10ft) eventually.

PROPAGATION
By semi-ripe cuttings taken in summer and rooted in a free-draining, soil-based compost, preferably in a warm propagator.

PRUNING
None necessary.

PROBLEMS
None.

RECOMMENDED VARIETIES
There are variegated myrtles but these are truly less than hardy and not reliable outdoors other than in very mild areas.

Myrtus communis

NANDINA

Nandina domestica Sacred bamboo

❝Gardens in the oriental style have become very popular in the West in recent years but, apart from attempting to fathom the underlying philosophical concepts, the biggest problem has lain with trying to grow bamboos in climates for which they are unsuited. Much of the answer lies with this plant, unexpectedly a member of the Berberis family, which is a significant component of oriental gardens in its own right, but rather more importantly, would almost pass muster as a bamboo. ❞

Nandina domestica 'Firepower'

CARE
Mulch lightly with compost in autumn and early spring and give a balanced general fertilizer in spring.

FOLIAGE INTEREST
Large, evergreen, reddish-green leaves subdivided into numerous leaflets, strong red-orange autumn colours.

NON-FOLIAGE APPEAL
Arching panicles of small, white flowers in early summer. Red berries may be formed, especially after hot summers and also when groups of plants are close together, fruit production being enhanced by cross-pollination.

SUITABILITY AS HEDGING
None.

SITE AND SOIL
Light shade, and tolerates most except very heavy and wet soils.

HARDINESS
Very hardy, tolerating -20°C (-4°F).

SIZE
Will attain about 80 x 80cm (32 x 32in) after five years and then will slowly reach about 1.5 x 1.5m (5 x 5ft).

PROPAGATION
By division in spring, in much the same way as a herbaceous perennial.

PRUNING
None necessary except for the cutting back of old or winter-damaged shoots to soil level in spring.

PROBLEMS
None.

RECOMMENDED VARIETIES
The normal species is a worthy plant but the best colours are on some of the selected Japanese forms, although the commonest in Europe is the neat, compact New Zealand variety, 'Firepower'.

Osmanthus

❝Osmanthus isn't a name to trip readily off gardeners' tongues although the plants themselves are common enough in shrubberies. I can only conclude that most people don't buy them but inherit them from previous owners. Like so many good plants, they are oriental, most displaying attractive evergreen foliage with pretty if unspectacular flowers. They are all extremely easy to grow. ❞

FOLIAGE INTEREST
Evergreen, glossy, toothed or spiny leaves in varying colours and variegations.

NON-FOLIAGE APPEAL
Richly scented masses of small, tubular, white flowers.

SUITABILITY AS HEDGING
None.

SITE AND SOIL
Best in light shade although tolerates full sun to medium shade. Tolerates most except very heavy and wet soils.

HARDINESS
Very hardy, tolerating -20°C (-4°F).

SIZE
Attains about 1 x 1m (3 x 3ft) after four or five years, 4 x 4m (13 x 13ft) eventually, although *O. x burkwoodii* rather less than this.

CARE
Mulch in autumn and early spring and give a balanced rose fertilizer in spring.

PROPAGATION
By semi-ripe cuttings in late summer, rooted in a free-draining, soil-based compost in a covered cold frame.

PRUNING
None necessary.

OZOTHAMNUS

RECOMMENDED VARIETIES

Osmanthus x *burkwoodii,* fairly large, more or less rounded, leathery, dark green, toothed leaves, silvery beneath, masses of small, perfumed, white spring flowers. *O. heterophyllus*, small, holly-like glossy, spiny, dark green leaves, small clusters of scented, white flowers in autumn; 'Aureomarginatus', variegated-yellow leaf edges; 'Purpureus', purple leaves; 'Variegatus', cream-white leaf edges, few flowers.

Ozothamnus

❝Ozothamnus *is a medium-sized genus of Australian shrubby daisies; and being Australian, few of them are reliably hardy in Europe. But there are two important exceptions, both of which have neat, very compact and highly aromatic foliage, the perfume being particularly pronounced in warm and sheltered corners of the garden. Both types also have the added appeal of masses of pretty white or yellowish-coloured flowers.* ❞

CARE
Mulch in autumn and early spring and give a balanced rose fertilizer in spring.
PROPAGATION
By semi-ripe cuttings in summer, rooted in a slightly humus-rich, soil-based compost in a covered cold frame.
PRUNING
None necessary.
PROBLEMS
None.

FOLIAGE INTEREST
Evergreen, narrow, almost needle-like, dull green leaves, slightly woolly beneath.
NON-FOLIAGE APPEAL
Appealing spicy perfume, masses of small flowers in summer.
SUITABILITY AS HEDGING
None.
SITE AND SOIL Full sun to
light shade, and tolerates most except very heavy and wet soils.
HARDINESS Moderately hardy,
tolerating about -10°C (14°F).
SIZE Attains about 1m x 50cm
(3ft x 20in) after five years, about 2 x 2m (6 x 6ft) eventually.

RECOMMENDED VARIETIES

Ozothamnus ledifolius (kerosene weed), markedly sticky foliage giving off inflammable vapour (hence common name), flowers yellowish, tinged red. *O. rosmarinifolius*, rosemary-like leaves, flowers white.

Osmanthus x *burkwoodii*

PROBLEMS
None.

Ozothamnus rosmarinifolius

PHILADELPHUS

Philadelphus coronarius Mock Orange

❝Philadelphus, *the mock oranges, obtain their common name from the rich, supposedly orange-like fragrance of the flowers. Indeed, it is as flowering shrubs that they have achieved their popular reputation. And, by and large, their foliage appeal is pretty small. But there is one notable exception in the golden-leaved form of the rather variable southern European species,* Philadelphus coronarius. *This species takes pride of place, right in the eye-line of one of my most important garden beds and, quite beautifully, backs a small classical statue.* ❞

CARE
Mulch in autumn and early spring and give a balanced rose fertilizer in spring.

PROPAGATION
By semi-ripe cuttings in summer, rooted in a soil-based compost in a cold frame, by hardwood cuttings in winter, or by layering: it's often possible to find naturally rooted layers.

PRUNING
None necessary, but growth soon becomes congested so cut out around one-third of the oldest shoots in spring.

PROBLEMS
Aphids, but rarely serious.

RECOMMENDED VARIETIES
'Aureus', intensely yellow foliage in spring, gradually becomes more green as the season progresses.

FOLIAGE INTEREST
Deciduous, elongated oval, slightly toothed, yellow leaves, changing to green in late summer, sometimes with yellow autumn colour but this isn't a reliable feature.

NON-FOLIAGE APPEAL
Single, white, perfumed, early summer flowers but not very conspicuous against the pale leaves.

SUITABILITY AS HEDGING
None.

SITE AND SOIL
Light shade, may scorch in full sun. Tolerates most soils but best on rich, well-drained, more or less neutral loam.

HARDINESS
Very hardy, tolerating -20°C (-4°F).

SIZE
Will attain about 1.5 x 1m (5 x 3ft) after five years and about 3-4 x 3-4m eventually (10-13 x 10-13ft).

Phillyrea decora

❝*The olive family, Oleaceae, includes a good number of under-appreciated hardy shrubs and this Mediterranean species (sometimes now called* Osmanthus decorus) *is a typical example. It will never shine or take trophies but it makes a useful addition to mixed shrubberies where its unusually elongated leaves provide a welcome contrast to much of the other workaday vegetation.* ❞

RECOMMENDED VARIETIES
The normal species is the only commonly available form.

CARE
Mulch in autumn and early spring and give a balanced rose or general fertilizer in spring.

PROPAGATION
By semi-ripe cuttings in summer,

Philadelphus coronarius 'Aureus'

PHOTINIA

FOLIAGE INTEREST
Evergreen, narrowly elongated, dark green, rather leathery leaves.

NON-FOLIAGE APPEAL
Masses of small, fragrant, white flowers in early summer.

SUITABILITY AS HEDGING
Makes an attractive, none too dense, low hedge, especially in milder areas.

SITE AND SOIL Best in light shade but tolerates full sun. In almost all soils, but unsuitable for heavy wet soils and also chalky sites.

HARDINESS Moderately hardy, tolerating -15°C (5°F).

SIZE Will attain about 1.5 x 1m (5 x 3ft) after five years and about 3 x 3m (10 x 10ft) eventually.

Photinia x fraseri 'Red Robin'

rooted in a free-draining, soil-based compost in a cold frame.

PRUNING
None necessary, but when grown as a hedge should be clipped around mid-summer and again in early autumn.

PROBLEMS
None.

Photinia x fraseri

❝ *Most evergreen foliage shrubs have a similar appeal all year round; this, after all, is how they score over deciduous species. And* Photinia x fraseri *is something of an exception, however, for while it is a good enough plant for a shrubbery at any time, it really creates its biggest impact as the new growth unfurls in spring. Then it will light up the garden with its vivid, rich, reddish candles.* ❞

FOLIAGE INTEREST
Evergreen, elongated oval, slightly toothed, reddish leaves, intense red colour on young shoots in spring.

NON-FOLIAGE APPEAL
None.

SUITABILITY AS HEDGING
In mild areas, may be used for a relatively informal, decorative boundary.

SITE AND SOIL Light to moderate shade, preferably slightly dappled. In almost all soil but consistently best on a rich organic, slightly acid loam.

HARDINESS Moderately hardy, tolerating -10 to -15°C (14 to 5°F).

SIZE Will attain about 1 x 1m (3 x 3ft) after five years and about 4 x 4m (13 x 13ft) eventually.

RECOMMENDED VARIETIES
'Red Robin' is easily the best of the few varieties available, with truly vivid red early season growth, later mellowing to a reddish-bronze.

CARE
Mulch in autumn and early spring and give a balanced general fertilizer in spring.

PROPAGATION
By semi-ripe cuttings in a rather humus-rich, soil-based compost in a cold frame in summer.

PRUNING
Not necessary, but misshapen plants may be cut back in spring and will regenerate. When grown as a hedge, may be clipped lightly in early summer.

PROBLEMS
None.

PHYSOCARPUS

Physocarpus opulifolius

❝ *The Rosaceae has probably contributed more species of useful if, by and large, unspectacular foliage shrubs to the garden than most families. This one is no exception, no more spectacular than the general run, but probably among the rather less widely grown types. It is scarcely worth growing the normal green-leaved species, for which the epithet 'boring' might be a fair choice, but the golden-foliaged variants are decidedly pretty when used to off-set other plants with contrasting colours.* ❞

FOLIAGE INTEREST
Deciduous, medium-sized, toothed, more or less golden leaves.
NON-FOLIAGE APPEAL
Masses of white or pinkish flowers in early summer, attractive, peeling, greyish-brown bark, especially conspicuous in winter.
SUITABILITY AS HEDGING
None, other than in a very informal setting as a tall, relatively insubstantial screen.
SITE AND SOIL Best in light shade, and in almost all soils but rarely at its best on thin or highly alkaline ones.
HARDINESS Very hardy, tolerating -20°C (-4°F).
SIZE Will attain about 1.5 x 1.5m (5 x 5ft) after five years and about 3 x 3m (10 x 10ft) eventually, although 'Dart's Gold' may reach only half this size.

CARE
Mulch in autumn and early spring and also give a balanced general fertilizer in spring.
PROPAGATION
By semi-ripe cuttings in summer, rooted in a soil-based compost in a cold frame, by hardwood cuttings in winter, or by removal of artificial or natural layers.
PRUNING
Not really necessary, but plants will be neater if up to about one-third of the oldest shoots are cut back to soil level in spring.
PROBLEMS
None.

> **RECOMMENDED VARIETIES**
> 'Dart's Gold', rich golden foliage for much of the season; 'Luteus', leaves golden in spring but later becoming greenish.

Physocarpus opulifolius **'Dart's Gold'**

Pieris

❝ *Pieris is one of that group of evergreen shrubs in the family Ericaceae that are bread and butter to any gardener with acid soil, but objects of curiosity and admiration to those who garden on more chalky sites. And although the selected forms especially are fine foliage plants, they have almost equal merit as flowering shrubs. Indispensable is an over-used term, but for the shrubbery on acid soil, Pieris comes close to being just that.* ❞

CARE
Mulch in autumn and early spring, ideally with shredded conifer needles or other acidic compost, and give a balanced rose fertilizer in spring.
PROPAGATION
By semi-ripe cuttings in a fairly humus-rich, soil-based compost in a cold frame in summer, or by layering; it is usually possible to find naturally rooted layers.
PRUNING
None necessary.
PROBLEMS
None.

> **RECOMMENDED VARIETIES**
> Although there are fine varieties selected for flowering quality, much the best foliage form is *Pieris* 'Forest Flame', with vivid reddish, early-season growth, reminiscent in many ways of *Photinia*. One of the parents of this plant is *Pieris japonica* which is generally inferior in both flower and leaf appeal, but there is a pretty variant of it with white leaf edges called 'Variegata'.

PITTOSPORUM

FOLIAGE INTEREST
Evergreen, elongated, leathery, dark green leaves with vivid red new growth in spring.
NON-FOLIAGE APPEAL
Large hanging clusters of small cream-white, bell-shaped flowers in spring.
SUITABILITY AS HEDGING
None.
SITE AND SOIL
Light to moderate shade, preferably with shelter from cold wind, and in acidic, moist, organic soil not prone to waterlogging.
HARDINESS
Moderately hardy, tolerating -10 to -15°C (14 to 5°F).
SIZE
About 50 x 75cm (20 x 30in) after three years, 2 x 2m (6 x 6ft) ultimately.

Pieris japonica 'Variegata'

Pittosporum tenuifolium

❝ *If there is a flower arranger in your family, they will fall on a pittosporum almost faster than anything, for the delicate, long-lasting foliage of this beautiful New Zealand evergreen plant is part of their stock in trade. Unfortunately, the flower arranger in my own family doesn't have such an opportunity, for this is a shrub that requires a climate just a little more reliably gentle than I can offer.* ❞

FOLIAGE INTEREST
Evergreen, small, more or less oval, predominantly greyish-green leaves with wavy edges.
NON-FOLIAGE APPEAL
None.
SUITABILITY AS HEDGING
In mild areas, makes a good and very decorative informal screen.
SITE AND SOIL
Full sun or light shade with shelter from cold winds; a very good plant for coastal gardens. Tolerates most soils provided fairly rich and free-draining, but intolerant of very chalky sites.
HARDINESS
Fairly hardy, tolerating about -10°C (14°F).
SIZE
About 1.5-2 x 1m (5-6 x 3ft) after five years, about 6 x 2.5-3m (20 x 8-10ft) eventually in mild areas.

CARE
Mulch in autumn and early spring; give a balanced general fertilizer in spring.

Pittosporum tenuifolium 'Purpureum'

RECOMMENDED VARIETIES
The normal species has pretty, slightly curled, greyish-green leaves that contrast with very dark-coloured twigs. 'Purpureum' has leaves that become bronze-purple as the summer progresses; 'Wareham Gold' has golden leaves, the colour of which intensifies as they age; the hybrid 'Garnettii' is the loveliest of all with whitish leaf margins and scattered pinkish spots.

PROPAGATION
By semi-ripe cuttings in late summer, in a rich but free-draining, soil-based compost in a cold frame.
PRUNING
None necessary but, if grown as a hedge, clip twice a year, once around mid-summer and then again any time in early autumn.
PROBLEMS
None.

PRUNUS

Prunus x *cistena* Purple sand cherry

" *This is one of those rather anonymous purple-leaved shrubs with few outstanding features to distinguish it from numerous others. But it is reliable, and will offer some spring flowers as an added attraction. Unlike many similar plants, it will withstand clipping and can be usefully used as a hedge. I always think of it as one of those plants that may not greatly enrich your gardening life, but will seldom let you down. It is a humble, harmless plant.* "

CARE
Mulch in autumn and early spring and give a balanced rose fertilizer in spring.

PROPAGATION
By hardwood cuttings in winter or by layering, although they take a long time to root.

PRUNING
None necessary, but if grown as a hedge, clip in mid-summer and then again in early autumn.

FOLIAGE INTEREST
Deciduous, fairly small, elongated oval, dark reddish-purple leaves, reddish autumn colour.

NON-FOLIAGE APPEAL
Small whitish flowers before leaves open in spring.

SUITABILITY AS HEDGING
Makes a useful if rather open-textured ornamental hedge.

SITE AND SOIL
Full sun to light shade. Tolerates most soils but may be particularly feeble on dry sites.

HARDINESS
Very hardy, tolerating -20°C (-4°F).

SIZE
About 1 x 1m (3 x 3ft) after five years, about 2 x 2m (6 x 6ft) eventually.

RECOMMENDED VARIETIES
The normal hybrid is the only form available.

PROBLEMS
None.

Prunus x *cistena*

Prunus laurocerasus Laurel, Cherry laurel

" *In my account of the bay (p.84), I've already referred to the confusion that I experience over which laurel is which; well, this one is the laurel of big hedges and Victorian parsonage gardens. It is also the one that has been tarred with the brush of boredom that seems to touch so much of nineteenth-century gardening. In its basic form, it certainly isn't the most beautiful of shrubs; useful, yes, but beautiful, no. And yet there are selected forms that are every bit as striking as most other easily grown evergreens.* "

FOLIAGE INTEREST
Evergreen, large, elongated oval, glossy green leaves.

NON-FOLIAGE APPEAL
Elongated clusters of small white flowers in spring; abundant on some varieties.

SUITABILITY AS HEDGING
Makes a large, dense, effective and fairly attractive hedge.

SITE AND SOIL
Full sun to deep shade, and in almost any soil although least successful on very alkaline sites.

HARDINESS
Very hardy, tolerating -20°C (-4°F).

SIZE
About 3 x 3m (10 x 10ft) after five years, about 6-8 x 5m (20-25 x 16ft) eventually.

RECOMMENDED VARIETIES

'Castlewellan', slightly twisted, white-speckled leaves, upright habit; 'Magnoliifolia' (sometimes known as 'Latifolia'), leaves very large, glossy, dark green, reminiscent of *Magnolia grandiflora*; 'Otto Luyken', elongated leaves, spreading, low-growing habit, good flowers; 'Rotundifolia', broader, paler green leaves, one of the neatest varieties for hedges; 'Variegata', cream and white leaf blotches; 'Zabeliana', narrow light green leaves and spreading, ground-cover habit.

Prunus laurocerasus 'Otto Luyken'

CARE

Mulch in autumn and early spring and also give a balanced general fertilizer in spring.

PROPAGATION

By semi-ripe cuttings in a soil-based compost in a cold frame in summer.

PRUNING

None necessary but may be clipped in mid-summer and again in early autumn when grown either as a specimen or as a hedge. Unfortunately, however, its large leaves are soon rendered unsightly by clipping and may tend to discolour when sliced; so, in an ideal world, pruning and shaping should be done with secateurs not shears.

PROBLEMS

None.

Prunus lusitanica
Portugal laurel

❝ *This is the third of the common types of garden laurel, arguably the most attractive but, by and large, the least often seen. It is, I always think, a plant for the more formal garden, and looks at its best when clipped neatly to form symmetrical topiary. Some of the finest and most impressive specimens that I know are neatly trimmed standards growing in large terracotta pots.* ❞

Prunus lusitanica

FOLIAGE INTEREST

Evergreen, fairly small, neat, narrowly elongated, dull green leaves with reddish stalks.

NON-FOLIAGE APPEAL

Elongated clusters of small, perfumed, white flowers in early summer, but not present on closely clipped specimens.

SUITABILITY AS HEDGING

Useful as a screen in any situation not exposed to cold winds.

SITE AND SOIL Full sun to deep shade, a good plant for coastal gardens, and in almost any soil although least successful on very dry sites.

HARDINESS Hardy, tolerating about -15°C (5°F).

SIZE About 1 x 1m (3 x 3ft) after five years, up to 10 x 7m (30 x 23ft) or even more eventually in very mild areas.

CARE

Mulch in autumn and early spring and give a balanced general fertilizer in spring.

PROPAGATION

By semi-ripe cuttings in a soil-based compost in a cold frame in summer.

PRUNING

None necessary, but clip formal shrubs in mid-summer and early autumn.

PROBLEMS

None.

RECOMMENDED VARIETIES

The normal species is the one to choose for most formal situations but there is a very pretty, slightly less hardy and slightly more open-textured variety, 'Variegata', with white or pinkish leaf edges.

PRUNUS

Prunus triloba Flowering almond

❝ *From a foliage standpoint, the Chinese* Prunus triloba *is one of the more unusual members of the genus in its possession of three-lobed rather than oval or oblong leaves. Like most spring-flowering deciduous species, it is usually considered simply as just another flowering cherry, but I would grow it for foliage interest too, and it is especially attractive when planted against a warm wall.* ❞

CARE

Mulch in autumn and early spring and give a balanced rose fertilizer in spring.

RECOMMENDED VARIETIES

The normal species will be the only one usually seen although there are one or two selected blossom variants.

PROPAGATION

Most easily by layering although can also be propagated from semi-ripe cuttings in a soil-based compost in a cold frame in summer.

PRUNING

None necessary, although the oldest shoots should occasionally be cut out in spring.

PROBLEMS

None.

FOLIAGE INTEREST

Deciduous, medium-sized, curiously three-lobed, mid-green leaves, yellow autumn colour.

NON-FOLIAGE APPEAL

Double, pink 'cherry' flowers before leaves open in spring.

SUITABILITY AS HEDGING

None.

SITE AND SOIL

Full sun to moderate shade, and in almost any soil although least successful on very dry sites.

HARDINESS

Hardy, tolerating about -15°C (5°F).

SIZE

About 1 x 1m (3 x 3ft) after five years, up to 4 x 3m (13 x 10ft) eventually.

Prunus triloba

RHODODENDRON

Rhododendron

❝ *The genus* Rhododendron *is one of the great glories of the botanical world. They are plants that just can't fail to impress by their beauty and, with the larger species, their sheer majesty. And this is true whether they are growing neatly on your rock garden or if you have been one of the lucky few to see them growing wild, clothing Himalayan hillsides. And I would be the first to admit that the real glory of the* rhododendron *is in its flowers. To think of rhododendrons as foliage plants is a more unusual concept and, whilst any massed planting of them certainly offers a great deal of green leaf, it is by and large only the really giant-leaved species that are worthy of growing on foliage account alone. You will need a big garden, an acid soil and a very mild climate, but you will be the envy of gardeners everywhere.* ❞

FOLIAGE INTEREST
Evergreen, ranging from medium-sized to enormous, glossy green leaves with felt-like indumentum beneath.

NON-FOLIAGE APPEAL
Beautiful flowers in various colours and in large clusters, generally in spring.

SUITABILITY AS HEDGING
None.

SITE AND SOIL
Light to moderate shade; some will tolerate full sun but are generally best as woodland plants. Best in deep, acidic, organic soil, moist but not prone to waterlogging, intolerant of any alkalinity.

HARDINESS
Varies with species from fairly hardy to very hardy, the larger types tolerating about -5 to -10°C (23 to 14°F) and the smaller ones -20°C (-4°F).

SIZE
Varies from an ultimate size of about 1 x 1m (3 x 3ft) for *R. yakushimanum* to 10 x 5m (30 x 16ft) for *R. sinogrande*.

Rhododendron ponticum 'Variegatum'

CARE
Mulch in autumn and early spring with compost, preferably of acidic material such as chopped conifer needles, and give a balanced rose fertilizer in spring.

RECOMMENDED VARIETIES
Rhododendron arboreum, large, mid-green leaves, reddish-brown beneath, flowers red, pink or white. *R. falconeri*, very large, mid-green, deeply ribbed leaves with felt-like, reddish-brown indumentum beneath, huge cream flowers. *R. fulvum*, large, very glossy green leaves with brown-red indumentum beneath, pink flowers. *R. grande*, very large, glossy dark green leaves, brownish-white beneath, huge white flowers. *R. sinogrande*, enormous, glossy dark green leaves (up to 75cm (30in) long), buff indumentum beneath, huge cream flowers. *R. yakushimanum*, a dwarf species up to about 1m (3ft) high, with narrow, dark green leaves with reddish-brown indumentum beneath, pink-white flowers. *R. ponticum* 'Variegatum', a form of the common naturalized rhododendron with whitish leaf margins, also has purple flowers; out of hundreds of varieties and species this is one of the very few variegated rhododendrons.

PROPAGATION
Difficult from cuttings and achieved most satisfactorily by layering.

PRUNING
None necessary; removal of dead flower heads is an advantage in encouraging the development of new flower buds but is clearly impractical on very large plants.

PROBLEMS
Various leaf spots and blotches, mildew.

ROSMARINUS

Rosmarinus officinalis Rosemary

" *Everyone knows rosemary as a shrubby kitchen-garden herb with small blue flowers, but I'm surprised how infrequently it is considered as a foliage plant. Yet it makes an excellent low hedge and responds well to close clipping, as well as forming an attractive specimen in a mixed shrub planting. It is a worthy component of any garden shrubbery provided it isn't allowed to romp away to become leggy and shapeless.* **"**

CARE
Mulch lightly in autumn and early spring, preferably with compost, and give a balanced rose fertilizer in spring.

PROPAGATION
By semi-ripe cuttings in early summer,

FOLIAGE INTEREST
Evergreen, small, almost needle-like, pleasantly aromatic bluish-green leaves.

NON-FOLIAGE APPEAL
Blue or, in some forms, white or pink flowers.

SUITABILITY AS HEDGING
Makes a good, neat, medium-height hedge.

SITE AND SOIL
Full sun to light shade. Tolerates most soils that are not very heavy, waterlogged or of extreme acidity or alkalinity.

HARDINESS
Very hardy, tolerating at least -20°C (-4°F).

SIZE
Most varieties will attain their maximum height of about 1.5-2m (5-6ft) after about five years.

RECOMMENDED VARIETIES

As foliage plants, the variation comes principally from the growth habit although there are forms with variegated foliage: 'Aureus', yellow-flecked leaves; 'Miss Jessop's Upright', erect habit; 'Prostratus', more or less prostrate habit.

---

struck in a soil-based compost, preferably in a warm spot.

PRUNING
At the least, cut out the oldest third of the shoots in spring and, if grown as a hedge, clip first around mid-summer and then again in early autumn.

PROBLEMS
None.

Rosmarinus officinalis

Rubus tricolor

" *This Chinese ornamental relative of the bramble is often seen clothing motorway embankments or industrial estates. But it is a useful if unspectacular garden plant, too, when used as ground cover in slightly wilder places; and although perfectly hardy, it is especially valuable in milder areas where it will remain more or less evergreen.* **"**

FOLIAGE INTEREST Semi-evergreen or evergreen, trifoliate, dark green leaves with reddish tints, whitish beneath.

NON-FOLIAGE APPEAL
Sparse, single, white flowers in summer.

SUITABILITY AS HEDGING
None.

SITE AND SOIL Full sun to moderate shade, and tolerates most soils provided they are not very heavy or waterlogged.

HARDINESS Very hardy, tolerating at least -20°C (-4°F) but will be severely browned and defoliated by very cold winds.

SIZE Will attain about 75cm x 1.5m (30in x 5ft) after about five years and perhaps double this spread eventually.

CARE
Mulch in autumn and early spring at least until well established, and give a balanced general or rose fertilizer in spring.

PROPAGATION
Easiest by layering or, easier still, by removal of naturally rooted layers.

RUSCUS

Rubus tricolor

FOLIAGE INTEREST
Evergreen, small, pointed, leaf-like stems (cladodes).

NON-FOLIAGE APPEAL
Red, berry-like fruits in autumn on female plants.

SUITABILITY AS HEDGING
None.

SITE AND SOIL Moderate to deep shade; generally unsatisfactory in full sun. In almost any soil; usefully very tolerant of dryness – very few other plants will grow in dry shade.

HARDINESS Very hardy, tolerating at least -20°C (-4°F).

SIZE Attains about 50 x 50cm (20 x 20in) in five years and around 1.2 x 1m (4 x 3ft) eventually.

PRUNING
In wilder areas, none necessary, but may also be cut back to the crown each year in early spring to encourage the attractive new foliage.

PROBLEMS
None.

RECOMMENDED VARIETIES
Generally, the normal species only is available although occasionally selected forms are offered and these are claimed to be more reliably evergreen.

Ruscus aculeatus Butcher's broom

❝ This is a plant seen more in student botany classes than in gardens, for it is certainly a structural oddity on two accounts. Firstly it is a member of the lily family, itself odd enough, but furthermore it also has only the most minute, scale-like, so-called leaves. What pass for leaves are in reality flattened stems. However, despite all of these peculiar features, this broom can find a place, albeit rather an unspectacular one, among other plants in a mixed shrubbery. ❞

CARE
Mulch in autumn and early spring and give a balanced general fertilizer in spring.

PROPAGATION
All but impossible from cuttings and best by removal of naturally formed rooted suckers.

PRUNING
None necessary.

PROBLEMS
None.

RECOMMENDED VARIETIES
The normal species will be the form most likely to be seen but the sexes are borne on separate plants both, of course, being needed for fruits to form on the female. But unfortunately, plants are not sexed when sold. Occasionally a hermaphrodite variant is available and this circumvents the problem.

Ruscus aculeatus

RUTA

Ruta graveolens Rue

❝ The Mediterranean rue is one of those plants that straddles the boundary between true woody shrubs and shrubby herbaceous perennials, but I have no hesitation in including it here because its foliage really is quite unlike anything else. And while seen most commonly in herb gardens, it can provide a very useful foil to other plants in mixed borders too. ❞

CARE
Mulch in autumn and early spring and give a balanced rose fertilizer in spring.

PROPAGATION
By semi-ripe cuttings taken in summer and rooted in a light, soil-based compost in a cold frame.

FOLIAGE INTEREST
Evergreen, rather finely divided, markedly bluish-green leaves.

NON-FOLIAGE APPEAL
Clusters of small yellow flowers at shoot tips in summer.

SUITABILITY AS HEDGING
None.

SITE AND SOIL Full sun, and tolerates most soils but best in light, free-draining but moderately rich sites.

HARDINESS Hardy, tolerating around -15°C (5°F).

SIZE Attains maximum height of approximately 75 x 60cm (30 x 24in) after a period of about two or three years.

RECOMMENDED VARIETIES
The normal species is widely available but two named forms are also frequently seen: 'Jackman's Blue', particularly well-coloured bluish foliage and generally speaking a more compact shape; 'Variegata', whitish leaf variegation, but as with most variegated plants, slightly more tender.

PRUNING
Remove two or three shoots to soi level each spring to encourage new and vigorous growth and, if necessary, the shrub can be trimmed lightly to shape in early summer.

PROBLEMS
None.

Salix Willow

❝ What do willows mean to you? Catkins in the spring, large trees, the roots of which invade your drains, pastoral scenes on river banks, or the raw material of traditional baskets? The huge genus Salix, with its 300 or so species, can supply all of these. But it can also offer a range of interesting plants that are worth growing principally for their leaf appeal, and, while none have exactly spectacular foliage, the characteristic willow leaf-shape can be a valuable component of almost any garden. Although the range in size and appeal is considerable, all of the willows that I include here require similar cultural conditions. ❞

Ruta graveolens 'Variegata'

SALIX

FOLIAGE INTEREST
Deciduous, oval to narrowly elongated, mainly green leaves.
NON-FOLIAGE APPEAL
Variously coloured and shaped, mainly upright catkins in spring.
SUITABILITY AS HEDGING
None.
SITE AND SOIL
Full sun to light or moderate shade, and in almost any soil types, but these shrubs are especially useful for their tolerance of waterlogged conditions.
HARDINESS
Very hardy, tolerating at least -20°C (-4°F).
SIZE
Varies widely; dwarf species will very slowly attain about 50 x 50cm (20 x 20in), medium-sized forms about 4 x 3m (13 x 10ft), and taller forms up to 6 x 5m (20 x 16ft); generally, the larger the ultimate size among willows, the faster they grow.

Salix exigua

CARE
Mulch in autumn and early spring; give a balanced general fertilizer in spring.
PROPAGATION
Probably the easiest of all shrubs to root from cuttings, and most readily achieved by hardwood cuttings in a soil-based compost in a cold frame in winter.

PRUNING
None necessary and on the smaller species none should be done. On larger shrubby willows it is wise to cut back at least a proportion of the shoots to soil level each spring, and if the plants become too large and unkempt then they may be cut back totally and will regenerate with ease.
PROBLEMS
Leaf spots, various leaf-attacking insects.

RECOMMENDED VARIETIES
Salix alba 'Argentea', (silver willow), medium-sized, elongated, silvery leaves, tall, fairly upright habit, yellow catkins. *S. x boydii*, small, rounded, greyish leaves, dwarf, extremely slow-growing, occasional greyish catkins. *S. exigua* (coyote willow), very narrowly elongated, silvery leaves, medium-sized, upright habit, small yellow catkins. *S. gracilistyla* 'Melanostachys', medium-sized, oval, dark green leaves, tall, upright habit, black catkins with red stamens. *S. lanata* (woolly willow), small, rounded, silvery, woolly leaves, dwarf, very slow-growing, small yellowish catkins. *S. magnifica* (magnolia-leaved willow), large, oval, magnolia-like, mid-green leaves, medium-sized, upright habit, slow-growing, yellow catkins. *S. phylicifolia* (tea-leaved willow), rounded, bright green leaves, yellow autumn colour, medium-sized, spreading habit, yellow catkins. *S. purpurea* 'Nana', very small, narrowly elongated, purplish leaves, fairly small, upright habit, small, silvery-purple catkins.

Salix alba 'Argentea'

Salix lanata

SAMBUCUS

Sambucus Elder

❝Sambucus nigra, *the elderberry, has a place in my affections for it was the first tree that I ever climbed as a child. We had a small group of them in one of the wilder parts of our garden, but I must confess that my liking for the normal, native species is for that sentimental reason alone, as it certainly has nothing to commend it as a garden plant. And indeed, for many gardeners, it is merely a woody weed. But there are a few rather attractive foliage variants and indeed a closely related species that combine to elevate the elders into an altogether better class.* ❞

RECOMMENDED VARIETIES

Sambucus nigra, common elder, 'Aurea', golden-yellow leaves; 'Laciniata', finely divided, fern-like leaves; 'Marginata', leaves with silvery-white edges; 'Pulverulenta', leaves with white streaks and blotches; 'Purpurea', leaves deep greenish-purple. *S. racemosa* 'Plumosa Aurea', finely divided golden leaves.

CARE
Mulch in autumn and early spring and give a balanced general fertilizer in spring.

PROPAGATION
Probably easiest by hardwood cuttings in winter in a soil-based compost in a cold frame, but also by semi-ripe cuttings in similar conditions in summer.

PRUNING
There are two ways to approach this: cut back the oldest third of the shoots

FOLIAGE INTEREST
Deciduous, variously divided, green, variegated, golden or purple leaves.

NON-FOLIAGE APPEAL
Masses of scented, white blossom in summer followed by black or red fruits.

SUITABILITY AS HEDGING
None.

SITE AND SOIL
Light to moderate shade; all golden-foliaged forms will scorch severely in full sun; they also need shelter from cold winds. Almost any soil, tolerant of considerable wetness and dryness.

HARDINESS
Very hardy, tolerating -20°C (-4°F) but liable to be damaged by very cold winds.

SIZE
With annual pruning to soil level, will attain about 2 x 1m (6 x 3ft) during each year; with selective pruning, will attain about 3 x 2m (10 x 6ft) within about five years.

Sambucus racemosa **'Plumosa Aurea'**

to soil level each spring to produce plants of the maximum size but that generally have rather smaller leaves. Alternatively, cut the entire plant back to soil level in spring to produce the best foliage, although the shrub will be smaller overall and will have little flower and fruit appeal.

PROBLEMS
Aphids.

SANTOLINA

Santolina Cotton lavender

❝Santolina *is the classic Mediterranean herb, with greyish or silvery leaves, an aroma that you may or may not take to, and a requirement for sun and light soil. But it has long had an important ornamental appeal too and has played second place only to dwarf box as the favoured edging for knot gardens and similar formal plantings.* ❞

FOLIAGE INTEREST
Evergreen, very tiny green to silvery leaves, closely packed on to finely divided shoots.

NON-FOLIAGE APPEAL
Small, button-like, yellow flowers in summer.

SUITABILITY AS HEDGING
Good as low edging for formally planted herb gardens or similar areas.

SITE AND SOIL Full sun, in light, free-draining soil, intolerant of heavy or waterlogged sites.

HARDINESS Hardy, tolerating around -15°C (5°F).

SIZE Will attain its full height of about 50 x 75cm (20 x 30in) within four or five years.

CARE
Mulch lightly with compost in autumn and early spring and give a balanced general fertilizer in spring.

PROPAGATION
By semi-ripe cuttings in late summer, rooted in a light soil-based compost, preferably in a covered propagator.

PRUNING
Most effectively by trimming lightly in

RECOMMENDED VARIETIES

Santolina chamaecyparissus, the normal species is the most commonly offered but there are also some selected forms available, 'Lambrook Silver' being the best for foliage, with its attractive silvery leaves. *S. pinnata* ssp. *neapolitana*, more feathery whitish-silver shoots. *S. virens*, feathery, bright green shoots.

Santolina pinnata neapolitana

Santolina chamaecyparissus

late spring, cutting just above the base of the previous season's growth.

PROBLEMS
None.

SENECIO

Senecio

❝I'm very fond of daisies, which is probably just as well in view of the fact that their family, the Compositae, is one of the largest in the plant kingdom. But it is their characteristic flowers that embody much of the group's appeal, and rather few among the hardy species can justifiably be grown for their foliage interest alone. But among them are a few silvery leaved, southern-hemisphere varieties that, whilst chosen primarily for their flowers, have an enduring leaf attraction too. The following plants are the 'traditional' senecios, although it should be added that some of them are now housed in the medical-sounding genus Brachyglottis. ❞

FOLIAGE INTEREST
Evergreen, silvery, often woolly leaves.
NON-FOLIAGE APPEAL
Medium-sized, white or yellow, typically daisy-like flowers in summer.
SUITABILITY AS HEDGING
None.
SITE AND SOIL Full sun or very light shade, tolerant of salt spray and good plants for coastal gardens. Tolerates most soils, but best in free-draining, moderately rich types, intolerant of heavy waterlogged sites. Moderately hardy, tolerating -15°C (5°F).
SIZE Will attain maximum size of about 1-1.5 x 1-1.5m (3-5 x 3-5ft) after about four years.

Senecio 'Sunshine'

CARE
Mulch lightly in autumn and early spring and also give a balanced rose fertilizer in spring.
PROPAGATION
By semi-ripe cuttings in summer, rooted in a free-draining, soil-based compost in a well-ventilated cold frame. Relatively young plants can also sometimes be divided in spring, much like a herbaceous perennial.
PRUNING
Trim lightly with shears in spring, although overgrown plants may be trimmed rather harder as they will usually regenerate fairly well from the old wood.
PROBLEMS
Aphids and fungal leaf spots.

RECOMMENDED VARIETIES
Senecio (syn. *Brachyglottis*) 'Sunshine', medium-sized, oval, greyish-silver leaves, with yellow flowers in summer. This plant is still sometimes called S. (syn. B.) *greyi*, although in reality that is a rarer, rather different species. *S. viravira* (also called *S. leucostachys*), medium-sized, finely divided, densely woolly, whitish-silver leaves, white flowers in summer.

Skimmia

❝More people probably complain to me about their failure with skimmias than with almost any other easily grown evergreen shrub. I suppose the commonest complaint concerns its failure to set berries, something easily explained by an incorrect choice of varieties. But a close second comes disappointment with what should be fine, dark green foliage but which is more often insipid and yellowing. In these instances, incorrect positioning is almost always responsible. ❞

CARE
Mulch in autumn and early spring and give a balanced rose fertilizer in spring.
PROPAGATION
By semi-ripe cuttings in summer, rooted in a free-draining, soil-based compost in a closed cold frame, or by hardwood cuttings similarly in a cold frame in winter.
PRUNING
None necessary, but old plants will

SOPHORA

FOLIAGE INTEREST
Evergreen, more or less elongated, dark green, leathery leaves.

NON-FOLIAGE APPEAL
Small white or yellowish flowers in spring, sometimes preceded by attractively coloured buds, rich red berries on female forms.

SUITABILITY AS HEDGING
None.

SITE AND SOIL
Light to moderate shade, foliage yellows unappealingly in full sun, and best in fairly rich, moist, organic soils. Intolerant of dry, shallow or alkaline soils which also result in feeble foliage. Hardy, tolerating -15° to -20°C (5°F to -4°F).

SIZE
Will attain maximum size of about 1-1.5 x 1-1.5m (3-5 x 3-5ft) after about four years.

Skimmia laureola

regenerate fairly well if up to one third of the oldest shoots are cut back to soil level in spring.

PROBLEMS
None.

RECOMMENDED VARIETIES
Skimmia japonica, evergreen, elongated-oval, rather large, leathery, dark green leaves, paler beneath, small white flowers in spring, berries on female varieties. *S. laureola*, evergreen elongated, leathery dark green leaves with strong aroma when crushed, low, spreading habit, small yellow-green flowers in spring, berries on female varieties.

Sophora tetraptera Kowhai

❝ If my garden was much more mild, this New Zealand member of the Leguminosae would be one of the first shrubs that I would plant. It always seems to me a classic example of a plant that looks best among its own kind, for in areas mild enough for Australasian plants in general it always seems to blend particularly well. As it is, I am denied both its most unusual fern-like evergreen foliage and its very pretty flowers. ❞

CARE
Mulch lightly with compost in autumn and early spring and give a balanced rose fertilizer in spring.

PROPAGATION
By semi-ripe cuttings in summer, rooted in a free-draining, soil-based compost in a closed cold frame, or from seed, although this is difficult to germinate if not obtained fresh and sown promptly in a propagator with bottom heat.

Sophora tetraptera

FOLIAGE INTEREST
Evergreen, small, more or less oval, fresh green leaves, arranged in fern-like or herringbone pattern along branches.

NON-FOLIAGE APPEAL
Masses of small, yellow, pea-like flowers in early summer.

SUITABILITY AS HEDGING
None.

SITE AND SOIL
Full sun and in free-draining, fairly rich soil, quite intolerant of heavy, wet or cold conditions. Moderately hardy, tolerating about -10°C (14°F) if shelter is given from cold winds.

SIZE
Out of its native climate, will attain about 1 x 1m (3 x 3ft) after about four years and 3-4 x 3-4m (10-13 x 10-13ft) eventually; in its native habitat will become a tree up to 10-12m (30-40ft) tall.

PRUNING
None necessary.

PROBLEMS
None.

RECOMMENDED VARIETIES
Normal species only is available.

SORBUS

Sorbus reducta

66 *Many sorbuses make fine garden plants, but most are trees, including the whitebeams and the large group of mountain ash types. These are most probably chosen more for their fruiting appeal than any foliage interest. This Chinese species is an exception, however, for it is a low-growing, ground-covering shrub with rather good foliage colour throughout both summer and autumn, as well as having attractive flowers and berries too.* 99

Sorbus reducta

CARE
Mulch in autumn and early spring and give a balanced rose or general fertilizer in spring.

PROPAGATION
By removal of natural suckers; the plant spreads readily by suckering.

FOLIAGE INTEREST
Deciduous, medium-sized, divided, rich green leaves with good orange-red autumn colour.

NON-FOLIAGE APPEAL
Masses of small white flowers in early summer and pinkish-white berries in autumn.

SUITABILITY AS HEDGING
None.

SITE AND SOIL
Full sun or light shade. Tolerates most soils, including fairly wet and fairly dry sites. Very hardy, tolerating -25°C (-13°F).

SIZE
Will attain about 25 x 50cm (10 x 20in) after five years and slowly reach about 50cm x 2m (20in x 6ft) eventually.

PRUNING
None necessary.

PROBLEMS
Leaf-attacking insects may cause unsightly holes or blisters in the foliage of the shrubs.

RECOMMENDED VARIETIES
Normal species only is available.

Spiraea japonica 'Goldflame'

Spiraea

66 *Spiraea is one of the commoner genera of northern-hemisphere, deciduous, rosaceous shrubs. There are several kinds in every garden centre and at least one in almost every garden. They are grown principally for their heads of tiny flowers, which range from white to lurid reds and pinks. But among this genus of extremely adaptable shrubs are a few with rather fine coloured foliage that are worth growing on this account alone.* 99

FOLIAGE INTEREST
Deciduous, fairly small, narrowly elongated, mid-green leaves, sometimes with toothed edges.

NON-FOLIAGE APPEAL
Heads of tiny pink, red or white flowers in summer.

SUITABILITY AS HEDGING
None.

SITE AND SOIL
Full sun to medium shade. Spiraeas tolerate most soils but are least successful on very dry sites. Very hardy, tolerating -25°C (-13°F).

SIZE
Spiraea japonica and *S. betulifolia* will attain about 75 x 50cm (30 x 20in) after five years and about 1.2 x 0.75m (4ft x 30in) eventually; *S. x vanhouttei* about double this.

CARE
Mulch in autumn and early spring and give a balanced rose or general fertilizer in spring.

PROPAGATION
Propagate by semi-ripe cuttings rooted

STEPHANANDRA

Spiraea vanhouttei

RECOMMENDED VARIETIES

Spiraea japonica (also called *S. x bumalda*) 'Anthony Waterer', some of the young leaves with pink and white variegation, red flowers; 'Golden Princess', golden-yellow leaves, pink flowers; 'Goldflame', orange leaves gradually become more golden towards autumn, red-pink flowers. *S. x vanhouttei*, dark green leaves, becoming purple as the season progresses. *S. betulifolia aemiliana*, more rounded (birch-like), bright green leaves with rich orange-red autumn colour, white flowers.

in a soil-based compost in a cold frame in early summer, or by hardwood cuttings in a cold frame in winter.

PRUNING

Differs with variety. Those that flower before midsummer should be pruned immediately after flowering: cut back the oldest third of the shoots to soil level. Those that flower after midsummer should be pruned in early spring: cut back all of the shoots to 20-25cm (8-10in) above soil level.

PROBLEMS

None.

Stephanandra incisa 'Crispa'

❝ *You can almost regard* Stephanandra *as being a deciduous ground-cover shrub that is as effective in winter, when leafless, as it is in the summer, for it makes such a congested mound of twigs that the soil is no more visible through it than if it were in full leaf. But this is a book on foliage plants, so it is the virtue of the leaves that really should be extolled. These are small, attractive and neat with fine autumn colour. And you can't ask much more than that, although there are pretty flowers too.* **❞**

CARE

Mulch in autumn and early spring, (at least until well established; it will soon become impossible to apply mulch if a massed ground-cover planting is made) and give a balanced rose or general fertilizer in spring.

Stephanandra incisa 'Crispa'

FOLIAGE INTEREST

Deciduous, small, divided mid-green leaves (rather reminiscent of *Crataegus*) with good orange autumn colour.

NON-FOLIAGE APPEAL

Heads of small cream-white flowers in summer.

SUITABILITY AS HEDGING

None.

SITE AND SOIL Full sun or

light shade. Tolerates most soils but least successful on dry sites. Very hardy, tolerating -20°C (-4°F).

SIZE Will attain about 50 x 75cm

(20 x 30in) after five years and about 1-1.5 x 1-1.5m (3-5 x 3-5ft) eventually.

PROPAGATION

By removal of naturally rooted layers, by artificial layering or by hardwood cuttings rooted in soil-less compost in a cold frame in winter.

PRUNING

None necessary, but plants may be thinned out by cutting some shoots back to soil level in spring.

PROBLEMS

None.

RECOMMENDED VARIETIES

My recommendation is for the ground-covering variety 'Crispa', in which the foliage plays the most important part. The normal species is a much taller, more vigorously growing shrub, worthy of a garden place perhaps on floral merit or as a much less neat ground cover.

SYMPHORICARPOS

Symphoricarpos orbiculatus

❝Symphoricarpos *is a North American and oriental genus of relatively unexciting but useful shrubs, the common names (of those that possess them) all ending in 'berry'. And by and large, this sums up their appeal, for the large, spherical white or pinkish fruits tend to remain conspicuously on the plants through the winter. But this species is something of an exception, for it has two variegated forms that are worth growing for their foliage alone.* ❞

FOLIAGE INTEREST
Deciduous, small, rounded, dull green leaves, some red-orange autumn colour.

NON-FOLIAGE APPEAL
Large, rounded, pinkish-white fruits in autumn, gradually turning reddish.

SUITABILITY AS HEDGING
Scarcely good enough on its own but rather attractive as part of a mixed screen-planting.

SITE AND SOIL
Full sun (normal species will tolerate deep shade but leaf variegation disappears under these conditions). Tolerates most soils and usefully tolerant of dry conditions. Very hardy, tolerating -20°C (-4°F).

SIZE
Will attain about 50 x 75cm (20 x 30in) after five years and about 1-1.5 x 1-1.5m (3-5 x 3-5ft) eventually.

S. orbiculatus **'Foliis Variegatis'**

CARE
Mulch in autumn and early spring and give a balanced rose or general fertilizer in spring.

PROPAGATION
By removal of naturally rooted suckers, by semi-ripe cuttings in summer, or by hardwood cuttings in winter rooted in soil-less compost in a cold frame.

PRUNING
Cut back the oldest third of the shoots to soil level in spring.

PROBLEMS
None.

RECOMMENDED VARIETIES
'Foliis Variegatis', leaves with yellow margins; 'Taff's Silver Edge', leaves with irregular silver-white margins.

Teucrium fruticans Shrubby germander

❝*I think that as a genus,* Teucrium *embraces some of the most boring of all the labiate herbs. The European wood sage,* Teucrium scorodonia, *for instance, isn't half the plant of the real sage, even in its variegated leaf forms. However, the Mediterranan* T. fruticans *is an exception to this, for it has good silver leaves. And whilst it might never make an outstanding specimen (it's rather too untidy for that), it can form a valuable component of a mixed planting for a dry and sunny garden.* ❞

FOLIAGE INTEREST
Evergreen, small, oval, greyish-green leaves with silver beneath on woolly stems.

NON-FOLIAGE APPEAL
Small blue flowers in summer.

SUITABILITY AS HEDGING
Rather pretty as a loose, informal screen in appropriately mild areas, especially by the sea.

SITE AND SOIL
Full sun with shelter from cold winds; good in coastal gardens. Best in light, free-draining, moderately rich soils, intolerant of heavy or waterlogged conditions. Moderately hardy, tolerating -10°C (14°F) if sheltered.

SIZE
Will attain about 1 x 1m (3 x 3ft) in five years, then double this eventually if unpruned.

VACCINIUM

CARE
Mulch lightly with compost in autumn and early spring and give a balanced rose or general fertilizer in spring.

PROPAGATION
By semi-ripe cuttings in summer, rooted in a free-draining, soil-based compost placed in a well-ventilated cold frame.

PRUNING
Lightly clip back the previous season's growth by about one-half in spring.

PROBLEMS
None.

RECOMMENDED VARIETIES
As a foliage plant, the normal species is as good as any; there are a few selected and named forms but these differ only in flower colour rather than foliage.

Vaccinium

❝ *Apart from* Rhododendron, Vaccinium *is perhaps the most classical acid-soil-loving of all shrub genera. It includes around 450 species, although relatively few are significant as garden plants. Among them are the acid-soil or heathland fruits such as blueberries, cranberries and bilberries, which are worth growing in appropriate conditions for their fruits. But many of them also have the added attraction of very fine autumn leaf colours. However, none are plants for small gardens because their period of real interest just isn't long enough but, given space, they will certainly turn some heads just before leaf-fall.* ❞

FOLIAGE INTEREST
Deciduous, small, oval to elongated, mid-green leaves with rich, mainly reddish autumn colour.

NON-FOLIAGE APPEAL
Bell-shaped white, pink or red flowers, mainly in early summer, followed by red or black, generally edible fruits.

SUITABILITY AS HEDGING
None.

SITE AND SOIL
Full sun or very light shade, most species require shelter from cold winds, in very acidic, moist but not waterlogged, highly organic soil. Very hardy, tolerating -20°C (-4°F)

SIZE
Varies widely throughout the genus. Of the two recommended species, *V. arctostaphylos* will attain about 75 x 75cm (30 x 30in) after five years and about 3 x 3m (10 x 10ft) eventually; *V. myrtillus* around one third of this.

CARE
Mulch in autumn and again in early spring with acidic compost; either chopped conifer needles or, better,

RECOMMENDED VARIETIES
Almost any of the deciduous species will offer good autumn colour and your choice will probably be dictated by which fruit you prefer. To pick out two that have special merit on grounds of autumn colour, I would opt for *Vaccinium arctostaphylos*, the Caucasian whortleberry, with narrowly elongated, dull green leaves with very good reddish-purple autumn colour, white summer flowers with flush of reddish-purple and black fruits, and *V. myrtillus*, the European bilberry or whortleberry, with small, oval, mid-green leaves on bright green stems, rich red autumn colour, pinkish flowers in early summer and black fruits.

conifer sawdust, and also give a balanced rose fertilizer in spring.

PROPAGATION
By semi-ripe cuttings in early summer or hardwood cuttings in winter, in an acidic, soil-less compost in a cold frame.

PRUNING
None necessary.

PROBLEMS
None.

Vaccinium myrtillus

VIBURNUM

Viburnum

❝ *Those who know viburnums speak very highly of them. Those who don't are missing a very large group of extremely useful and, in some instances, remarkably attractive shrubs in a very wide range of sizes. But I don't think that viburnums are ever pretty; they are too robust and tough for that, especially the evergreen forms. Among the 150 or so species, most of the best known of those grown in gardens are chosen for their flowers, and it is probably the winter-blooming species or hybrids like* Viburnum x bodnantense *that are the most familiar. But there remain a number, both deciduous and evergreen, that are worth growing for their foliage appeal alone.* ❞

FOLIAGE INTEREST
Deciduous (with good autumn colour) or evergreen, mainly fairly large, elongated, dark green leaves but with several variations.

NON-FOLIAGE APPEAL
Mainly small, white flowers, often in large, attractive heads in spring and summer but produced in winter in some species, and followed by red or black fruits in various seasons.

SUITABILITY AS HEDGING
Some species, such as *V. opulus*, make useful and attractive additions to informal mixed hedges.

SITE AND SOIL
Generally best in light shade but most will tolerate full sun and some medium to deep shade, too. In almost any soil, although a few species are less successful on very wet or very dry sites. Hardiness varies with species but all are at least moderately hardy, tolerating -10°C (14°F) and some are very hardy.

SIZE
Most viburnums will attain about 1 x 1m (3 x 3ft) after four or five years and 3-4 x 3-4 m (10-13 x 10-13ft) eventually, but ultimate sizes and growth rates vary considerably throughout the group so be sure to check label descriptions carefully.

CARE
Mulch in autumn and early spring and also give a balanced rose fertilizer in spring.

PROPAGATION
By semi-ripe cuttings in early summer or hardwood cuttings in winter, rooted in a soil-based compost in a cold frame.

PRUNING
None necessary.

PROBLEMS
None.

Viburnum acerifolium

Vibernum x hillieri

Viburnum davidii

Viburnum rhytidophyllum

RECOMMENDED VARIETIES

Viburnum acerifolium, deciduous, three-lobed (*Acer*-like), pale green leaves with rich red autumn colour, small white flowers in summer, red then purple-black fruits. *V. cylindricum*, evergreen, large, elongated, dull green leaves, pale green beneath, small white summer flowers, black fruits. *V. davidii*, evergreen, large, oval, leathery, glossy dark green leaves, small white flowers in early summer, bluish fruits (on female forms). *V. furcatum*, deciduous, large, oval, dull green leaves with orange-red autumn colour, large white flowers in spring, red then black fruits. *V. x hillieri*, evergreen, narrowly elongated, dark green leaves with orange flush, small white flowers in early summer, red then black fruits. *V. lantanoides* (also called *V. alnifolium*), deciduous, large, rounded, mid-green leaves with rich red autumn colour, large white flowers in early summer, red then purple-black fruits. *V. opulus* (guelder rose), deciduous, three- to five-lobed (*Acer*-like) pale green leaves with orange-red autumn colour, white lacecap- or snowball-style summer flowers, red fruits but lacking on snowball varieties such as 'Roseum' (syn. 'Sterile').
V. 'Pragense', evergreen, elongated, dark green leaves, white and woolly underneath, white flowers in early summer, red then black fruits. *V. rhytidophyllum*, evergreen, large, elongated, shiny dark green leaves with furrowed surface, greyish and woolly underneath, small cream flowers in spring, red then black fruits; 'Variegatum' is a fine form with white blotches on the leaves. *V. tinus* 'Variegatum', evergreen, small, broadly oval, dark green leaves with white variegation, silver-coloured underneath, small, white winter flowers, black fruits.

Viburnum lantanoides

VINCA

Vinca Periwinkle

" *After climbers for cold shady walls, the question I am asked most frequently is what plants can be grown for effective ground-cover that will thrive in dry shade. And while a number of herbaceous perennials will fill the bill (see* Best Shade Plants, *Book 3 of the series),* Vinca *always feature somewhere on my list. They aren't spectacular but they are reliable; and if you choose carefully, you will find some of the foliage variants are really rather pretty.* "

CARE

Mulch in autumn and early spring until well established; once a carpet of ground-cover has developed, mulching is all but impossible; give a balanced rose or general fertilizer in spring.

RECOMMENDED VARIETIES

Vinca major, medium-sized, elongated oval, shiny green leaves; 'Maculata', yellow blotch on leaves, pale blue flowers; 'Variegata', cream-white leaf variegation, blue-mauve flowers. *V. minor*, small, elongated oval, shiny green leaves; 'Aureovariegata', yellow leaf variegation, mauve-blue flowers; 'Argenteovariegata', white-cream leaf variegation, blue flowers.

PROPAGATION

Most readily by removal of naturally rooted layers, but also by semi-ripe cuttings in early summer, or by hardwood cuttings in winter, rooted in a soil-based compost in a cold frame.

PRUNING

None strictly necessary, but I find it advantageous to cut back fairly hard in spring, using either a pair of shears or a powered strimmer.

FOLIAGE INTEREST

Deciduous, small to medium-sized, elongated, pointed, pale green leaves.

NON-FOLIAGE APPEAL

Clusters of small, tubular, pink flowers in early summer.

SUITABILITY AS HEDGING

May be used among other shrubs as part of an informal ornamental screen.

SITE AND SOIL

Full sun to light shade, in almost all soils but least successful on very dry sites. Very hardy, tolerating -20°C (-4°F).

SIZE

Will attain about 1 x 1m (3 x 3ft) after about five years and slightly more than twice this eventually.

PROBLEMS

Rust can be seriously disfiguring and weakening on *V. major*.

Vinca minor 'Aureovariegata'

Vinca major 'Variegata'

WEIGELA

Weigela florida

Weigela *is another workhorse genus of reliable, if not exactly spectacular, flowering deciduous, oriental shrubs, rather poor shadows of their close relatives, the shrubby honeysuckles. Unfortunately, most of them have not merely unexciting but positively dismal foliage. There are a few exceptions in a small group of rather pretty variegated forms, however, one of which has become one of the most widely grown of all the shrubs that combine flower appeal with a variegated leaf.* "

FOLIAGE INTEREST
Evergreen, more or less elongated, shiny green leaves on long, trailing, ground-covering stems.

NON-FOLIAGE APPEAL
Blue or purplish flowers (white on some green-leaved varieties).

SUITABILITY AS HEDGING
None.

SITE AND SOIL
Full sun to deep shade, may be browned in very cold winds. In almost any soil, including dry, although less successful on very wet sites. Very hardy, tolerating -20°C (-4°F)

SIZE
V. major will attain about 50cm x 1m (20in x 3ft) and *V. minor* about 20 x 80cm (8 x 32in) in about four years, but groups of plants should be placed fairly close together to achieve the ground-covering effect.

CARE
Mulch in autumn and spring; give a balanced rose or general fertilizer in spring.

Weigela 'Florida Variegata'

PROPAGATION
Propagate by semi-ripe cuttings in late summer or hardwood cuttings in winter, rooted in a soil-based compost in a cold frame.

PRUNING
None necessary, but it is sensible to cut back the oldest third of the shoots to soil level in spring.

PROBLEMS
None.

RECOMMENDED VARIETIES
Weigela 'Florida Variegata', cream-white leaf edges, pink flowers; 'Aureovariegata', yellow leaf variegation with pink flush, pink flowers.

XANTHOCERAS

Xanthoceras sorbifolium

❝ This Chinese plant is a rarity, and not just because it is the only garden shrub with a name that begins with an X. It is also rarely seen, but I don't honestly know why for it is not particularly tender and not particularly difficult to grow. I suspect that the reason may be the same as with a number of other Chinese plants: that it will tolerate a pretty hard winter but will only flower reliably if this is followed by a good hot summer. Nonetheless, even if that does provide an explanation, it is no excuse because flowers or not, this shrub is a perfectly worthy species as a foliage plant alone. ❞

CARE
Mulch in autumn and early spring and also give a balanced rose fertilizer in spring.

PROPAGATION
Difficult from cuttings, although hard-wood cuttings in a free-draining soil-based compost in a cold frame in winter may be successful. It is also said to be easy to propagate from seed, but this appears to be of academic interest for I have never seen any seed offered for sale.

PRUNING
None necessary.

PROBLEMS
None.

RECOMMENDED VARIETIES
Normal species only is available.

FOLIAGE INTEREST
Deciduous, rather finely divided, somewhat fern-like, light green leaves with toothed leaflets and yellow autumn colour.

NON-FOLIAGE APPEAL
Medium-sized, tubular, white flowers with red centres in spring produced after a warm summer the previous year.

SUITABILITY AS HEDGING
None.

SITE AND SOIL Full sun to light shade, but must have shelter from cold winds; most successful as a wall shrub in cooler areas. In almost any soil and usefully tolerant of alkalinity. Moderately hardy, tolerating about -10°C (14°F).

SIZE Will attain about 1 x 1m (3 x 3ft) after five years and about 6 x 6m (20 x 20ft) eventually.

Xanthoceras sorbifolium

Yucca

❝ Surely everyone knows the Central American yucca, for there are few hardy plants of such characteristically spiky, succulent form. And because of this unique quality, it is greatly favoured by garden designers who happily blend it with the likes of Fatsia or large-leaved ivies. But it has a place in the more traditional formal garden too, where it is a particularly effective foliage subject for a large terracotta container. The flower spikes are spectacular when they develop, but you may have to wait a long time for them. If you have children, do take care when selecting a yucca for your garden: some varieties can have very sharp leaves and are best avoided. ❞

FOLIAGE INTEREST
Evergreen, sword-like, green or bluish-green leaves arising from a large rosette, either with or without a stem.

NON-FOLIAGE APPEAL
Tall spikes of white flowers in warm summers on established mature plants.

SUITABILITY AS HEDGING
None.

SITE AND SOIL Full sun, preferably with some shelter from cold winds. In almost any soils except heavy, wet and cold ones. Moderately hardy, tolerating about -10°C (14°F).

SIZE Will attain about 1 x 1m (3 x 3ft) after five years and about 6 x 6m (20 x 20ft) eventually.

ZENOBIA

CARE
Mulch lightly with compost in autumn and early spring, even in containers, and give a balanced rose or general fertilizer in spring.

PROPAGATION
Most satisfactorily by division or removal of offsets in spring. Yuccas may be raised from seed but the results will be variable and unpredictable, and the plants seldom as good as the selected named forms.

PRUNING
None necessary.

PROBLEMS
None.

Yucca gloriosa

RECOMMENDED VARIETIES
Yucca filamentosa, greyish-green leaves with cottony, thread-like fibres at edges; 'Bright Edge', yellow streaks along leaf edges; 'Variegata', white leaf edges.
Y. flaccida, bluish-green leaves with white fibrous edges, stemless; 'Golden Sword', yellow leaf edges.
Y. gloriosa, bluish-green leaves with needle-like tips: 'Variegata', leaves with yellow stripes.

Zenobia pulverulenta

❝ *One of the least well-known members of the Ericaceae, at least in Europe although it is seen fairly frequently in gardens in North America, where it originated. It is particularly attractive in autumn if interplanted with rhododendrons and other evergreen acid-soil shrubs when its fine autumn colours contrast well with their dark green foliage.* ❞

RECOMMENDED VARIETIES
Normal species only is available.

CARE
Mulch twice, once in autumn and again in early spring, preferably with acidic compost such as conifer sawdust or chopped conifer needles.

PROPAGATION
Easiest by layering but also by semi-ripe

FOLIAGE INTEREST
Deciduous, elongated-oval, dull green leaves with red-orange autumn colours.

NON-FOLIAGE APPEAL
Small, scented, white flowers in summer.

SUITABILITY AS HEDGING
None.

SITE AND SOIL
Full sun to moderate shade, in acidic, organic, moist but free-draining soil. Moderately hardy, tolerating about -15°C (5°F).

SIZE
Will attain about 50 x 50cm (20 x 20in) after five years and about 1.5 x 1.5m (5 x 5ft) eventually.

cuttings taken in early summer for rooting in an acidic soil-less compost in a cold frame.

PRUNING
None necessary.

PROBLEMS
None.

Zenobia pulverulenta

CONIFERS

Conifers

" *If one plant can be said to characterize the modern garden, it must be the conifer. For, although they have been grown and planted for centuries (witness the magnificent cedars and pines in many of our great public gardens), the second half of the twentieth century has seen an explosion in the range of varieties available. And, most importantly, the majority of these new forms are of much slower or more restricted growth than their forebears. In the wild, almost every conifer naturally grows to tree size, but the slow-growing, low, so-called dwarf conifers of modern gardens are shrubs in all but name. They are sports, mutants or aberrations,*

sometimes formed pathologically (some as witches' brooms, for instance, which are twiggy out-growths caused by various factors including virus and fungal infection), that have been seized on by nurserymen, propagated by vegetative means and then launched upon the gardening fraternity. But because conifers are not flowering plants, these dwarf forms can with justification be considered foliage shrubs, horticulturally if not strictly botanically.

Their appeal derives from the shape and form of their leaves (needles), the way that these are massed on the shoots, the colour of the needles and the overall form of the plant which may range from

fastigiate through weeping to completely prostrate, with conical, spherical and most other geometric shapes in between.

Unfortunately, so popular and extensive has the range of conifers now become that the varieties available at one nursery or garden centre may differ widely from those at another, especially among some of the dwarf forms. While I have given my personal choice of varieties, therefore (and have indicated those most likely to be encountered), I have also given general indications of the features offered by the main genera, in the hope that this will aid your selection even if my particular varietal suggestions are unavailable. "

CARE
Mulch in autumn and early spring; give a balanced general fertilizer in spring.

PROPAGATION
Conifers are extremely difficult to root from cuttings without the aid of the constantly moist environment provided by a misting facility, and it really is pointless for gardeners to try. Even commercially, many of the most choice varieties are grafted because they grow inadequately on their own roots if, indeed, they are even capable of developing a root system. In some cases, this seems to be because the dwarfing effect is brought about by virus contamination of the tissues, which in turn also affects rooting ability. Although many hedging conifers are raised easily from seed, almost no selected forms will come true.

Abies koreana

Juniperus horizontalis

PRUNING

When grown as hedges, conifers should be clipped at least twice each year. This is best done first just before mid-summer and then again in very early autumn. If the hedges are to become dense and attractive, it is also most important that clipping starts at a young age (see p.14). By and large, dwarf conifers grown as specimens need very little pruning (indeed, this is one of their merits), and merely cutting out wayward branches or removing the upright shoots that commonly appear on otherwise prostrate plants is all that should be needed.

PROBLEMS

Red spider mites and root decay fungi can be problematic.

FOLIAGE INTEREST

Evergreen (or rarely deciduous), abbreviated leaves (needles), sometimes densely crowded on branches.

NON-FOLIAGE APPEAL

Overall form; cones on a few species but rarely when young.

SUITABILITY AS HEDGING

Many taller-growing varieties make excellent dense screens and boundaries; few of the dwarf forms described here are suitable.

SITE AND SOIL
Full sun to light shade, preferably with shelter from cold winds, and generally intolerant of salt spray. Golden-foliaged forms may scorch in full sun but, conversely, tend to become green in too dense a shade. They tolerate most soils, although always best on well-drained, fairly rich soils and least successful on wet heavy soils; generally most satisfactory in slightly acid rather than slightly alkaline conditions. Hardiness varies, but most of those recommended here are hardy to moderately hardy, tolerating between about -10° and -20°C (14° and -4°F).

SIZE
Varies widely, but the indications I have given are of expected sizes after about 10 years' growth in good conditions.

CONIFERS

FINDING YOUR WAY AROUND
THE NAMES

Although all plants have scientific names based on Latin, dwarf conifers seem to have more names than most, and their varietal names also tend to be derived from Latin or Greek rather than from modern languages. While not an infallible guide, the name can usually be relied upon to describe the appearance pretty accurately. The following list gives the names and their meanings, in the hope that it will help in selecting appropriate varieties, especially when choosing conifers from catalogues:

Plant name

Alba	White
Argentea	Silver
Aurea	Golden
Brevifolia	Short-leaved
Columnaris	Columnar
Compacta	Compact
Densa	Dense
Glauca	Blue-green
Gracilis	Graceful
Fastigiata	With vertical branches
Filifera	Thread-like
Lutea	Yellow
Minima	Smallest
Nana	Dwarf
Obtusa	Rounded
Pendula	Pendulous with branches hanging down
Prostrata	Prostrate with branches spreading along the ground
Pygmaea	Small
Variegata	Variegated

Juniperis communis 'Compressa'

RECOMMENDED VARIETIES

The colour referred to is that of the needles, generally in summer unless I have stated otherwise, but it should be noted that the dormant buds in winter and the extending new shoots in spring may be extremely colourful. * An asterisk denotes the varieties most widely available.

Abies (silver firs), mainly pyramidal or Christmas-tree-like in overall form, usually with rather short stiff needles. The foliage colours include good green-, silver- and golden-leaved types, and among the dwarf forms are some fine prostrate varieties. Among the most notable species is *A. koreana*, the Korean fir, which probably produces cones at a younger age than any other common conifer. *A. balsamea* 'Nana' (f. *hudsonia* is almost identical), dark green, rounded, dense habit, 30 × 30cm (12 × 12in). *A. concolor* 'Compacta', silvery needles, turning dark green, irregular rounded habit, 75 × 75cm (30 × 30in). *A. koreana, dark green needles, silver beneath, pyramidal 1.5 × 1m (5 × 3ft) after five years, very slowly to 10m (30ft); 'Flava' has golden-yellow needles; 'Silberlocke' has twisted needles that reveal their silver undersides. *A. lasiocarpa* 'Compacta', rich silver-blue, densely pyramidal, 1m × 45cm (3ft × 18in). *A. nordmanniana* 'Golden Spreader', golden needles, at first more or less prostrate but later more rounded, 60 × 60cm (24 × 24in). *A. procera* 'Glauca Prostrata', bluish-silver needles, irregular, sprawling habit, 50cm × 1.2m (20in × 4ft).

Cedrus (true cedars), soft-foliaged, gracefully spreading or weeping plants with some good golden forms. *C. deodara* 'Golden Horizon', golden-yellow needles, more green in winter, more or less prostrate, 60cm × 2m (24in × 6ft).

Cephalotaxus (Japanese cowtail pine). *C. harringtonia* 'Fastigiata', dark green needles, dense fastigiate habit, 2m × 75cm (6ft × 30in).

Chamaecyparis (false cypress), needles very small and not obvious, shoots soft and frond-like, green or golden, a huge group of columnar, dome-shaped or conical plants, including important hedging varieties. *C. lawsoniana* 'Aurea Densa' golden yellow, dense, rounded habit, 45 × 30cm (18 × 12in); *'Ellwood's Pillar', dark blue-green, fairly dense, columnar, 75 × 30cm (30 × 12in); 'Gnome', blue-green, dense, rounded habit, 20 × 30 cm (8 × 12in); 'Green Globe', bright green, dense, rounded habit, 25 × 25 cm (10 × 10in); *'Minima Aurea', golden yellow, dense, more or less pyramidal, 60 × 30cm (24 × 12in); 'Pygmaea Argentea', blue-green with cream-white branch tips, rounded habit, 30 × 30cm (12 × 12in); 'Silver Threads', yellow-green with yellow specks, shortly columnar, 1m × 45cm (3ft × 18in). *C. obtusa* 'Nana Aurea', golden yellow, rather irregular spreading habit, 75 × 30cm (30 × 12in); *'Nana Gracilis', dark green, irregularly pyra-midal with arching twisted branches, 1m × 60cm (3ft × 24in); 'Nana Lutea', golden yellow, irregularly pyramidal, 60 × 45cm (24 × 18in). *C. pisifera* *'Filifera Aurea', golden, slender

stems, spreading pyramidal habit, 1 × 1m (3 × 3ft); 'Nana', dark green, dense, dome-shaped, 25 × 30cm (10 × 12in); 'Plumosa Compressa', bright yellowish-green, irregularly spreading, 15 × 25cm (6 × 10in).

Cryptomeria japonica (Japanese cedar), columnar or cone-shaped trees with fresh green needles, few dwarf forms. 'Sekkan-Sugi', yellow and green, broadly columnar, 2 × 1m (6 × 3ft).

x Cupressocyparis (Leyland cypress), I include this hybrid for the sake of completeness as it is probably the most commonly planted garden conifer, although it is certainly no shrub and is barely containable as a hedge. Other than in a few very exposed gardens as a useful windbreak, it is a plant that most gardeners can do without.

Cupressus (cypress) is similar to *Chamaecyparis* but with fewer dwarf forms, and I recommend it only for its taller-growing forms.

Juniperus (juniper), a huge group of varieties, some with prickly shoots of characteristic bluish-green, including many good and neat dwarf and prostrate forms. *J. chinensis*, 'Kuriwao Gold', yellow-ish-gold, rounded and spreading, 2 × 1.5m (6 × 5ft). *J. communis* *'Compressa', blue-green, dense, neatly columnar, perhaps my favourite dwarf conifer, 1.5m × 30cm (5ft × 12in); *'Depressa Aurea', golden yellow, more green in winter, more or less prostrate, 50cm × 1.5m (20in × 5ft); 'Green Carpet', dense, greenish-bronze, prostrate, 15cm × 1m (6in × 3ft).

CONIFERS

RECOMMENDED VARIETIES

(CONTINUED)

J. horizontalis 'Blue Chip', bluish-green, feathery shoots, prostrate, 30cm x 1.5m (12in x 5ft); 'Emerald Spreader', bright green, especially in summer, prostrate, 15cm x 2m (6in x 6ft); 'Prince of Wales', bright green, especially in summer, prostrate. *J. x media* 'Gold Sovereign', yellow-gold, spreading, umbrella-like, 75cm x 2m (30in x 6ft). *J. procumbens* 'Nana', bright green, prostrate, 25cm x 1.5m (10in x 5ft). *J. recurva* 'Densa', bright green, semi-prostrate, 40cm x 1m (16in x 3ft). *J. sabina* *'Tamariscifolia', bluish-green, neatly splayed branches, prostrate, 45cm x 1.5m (18in x 5ft). *J. squamata* *'Blue Carpet', very bluish-green, semi-prostrate, 45cm x 2m (18in x 6ft).

Larix (larch), although the pyramidal, deciduous larches, with their beautiful soft needles are my favourite conifers, sadly there are very, very few dwarf forms. *L. kaempferi* 'Nana', bright green, softly rounded habit, 50 x 50cm (20 x 20in).

Picea (spruce), the familiar British Christmas tree is the Norway spruce, *P. abies*, and typifies their form with its fairly short, rather prickly needles and pyramidal shape. There are some good golden- and bluish dwarf forms. *P. abies* 'Inversa', dark green, prostrate, 20cm x 1.5m (8in x 5ft); 'Nidiformis', dark green, upright with an inverted centre like a bird's nest, 50cm x 1m (20in x 3ft); 'Pygmaea', dark green, broadly pyramidal, 30 x 20cm (12 x 8in). *P. glauca* *'Alberta Globe', bright green,

dome-shaped; *albertiana* 'Conica', bright green, cone-shaped, 1m x 60cm (3ft x 24in); 'Laurin', smaller and slower-growing version of *albertiana* 'Conica', 30 x 15cm (12 x 6in). *P. mariana* 'Ericoides', rounded, compact, spreading, 45cm x 1m (18in x 3ft); 'Nana', bluish-green, rounded, 15 x 25cm (6 x 10in). *P. omorika* 'Nana', dark green, silvery beneath, rounded, 1m x 75cm (3ft x 30in). *P. pungens* *'Globosa', bright steely blue, irregularly rounded habit, 60 x 60cm (24 x 24in); *'Hoopsii', steel-blue, broadly conical, 2.5 x 1.2m (8 x 4ft); 'Procumbens' (also called 'Prostrata'), blue, irregularly semi-prostrate, 30 x 50cm (12 x 20in).

Pinus (pine), long-needled, in some instances very long-needled, and very beautiful but with relatively few dwarf forms. The groups within the genus are distinguished by the numbers of needles within each cluster – two, three or five. *P. contorta* (two-needled) 'Frisian Gold', golden yellow, irregularly rounded, 60 x 60cm (24 x 24in). *P. heldreichii leucodermis* (two-needled) 'Schmidtii', dark green, irregularly rounded, a lovely plant, 40 x 40cm (16 x 16in). *P. mugo* (two-needled) 'Mops', rather bright green, irregularly rounded, 75 x 75cm (30 x 30in), easily the best of several similar forms of this species. *P. strobus* (five-needled) 'Nana', bluish-green, irregularly rounded and spreading, 1.2m x 1.2m (4 x 4ft); 'Reinshaus', bluish-green, irregularly rounded, delightful, 75 x 75cm (30 x 30in). *P. sylvestris* (two-needled) 'Doone Valley', greenish-silver, irregularly rounded, 45 x 45cm (18 x 18in).

Taxus (yew), dark green trees of generally rounded and rather untypically coniferous form. Beautiful trees and the hedging plant par excellence but with rather few dwarf forms although with some lovely slow-growing fastigiate varieties. 'Fastigiata Aurea', golden, upright, columnar, stately, 2m x 60cm (6ft x 24in); 'Repandens', very dark green, spreading, semi-prostrate, 60cm x 1m (24in x 3ft); 'Standishii', golden, upright, columnar, 1.5m x 30cm (5ft x 12in).

Thuja (red cedars), small, rather soft, cypress-like needles, generally with pleasant aroma, typically narrowly pyramidal in shape. *T. occidentalis* 'Danica', bright green, turning more golden in winter, neatly rounded, 50 x 50cm (20 x 20in); 'Hetz Midget', green, turning more golden or bronze in winter, neatly rounded, 30 x 30cm (12 x 12in); *'Smaragd', bright green, narrowly columnar, 2.5m x 60cm (8ft x 24in); *'Sunkist', yellowish-gold, neatly pyramidal, 1.5 x 1m (5 x 3ft). *T. orientalis* *'Aurea Nana', beautiful, soft pale green, 75 x 45cm (30 x 18in). *T. plicata* 'Rogersii', dark golden yellow, neatly rounded, 45 x 45cm (18 x 18in).

Tsuga (hemlock), small, soft, cypress-like needles, typically narrowly pyramidal. *T. canadensis* 'Cole', dark green, neatly prostrate, 15cm x 1m (6in x 3ft); *'Jeddeloh', bright green, neat, low mounded habit with depressed centre, 45 x 60cm (18 x 24in).

Thuja orientalis **'Aurea Nana'**

Picea pungens

Pinus strobus **'Nana'**

INDEX

Page numbers in italic refer to the illustrations

Abies 123
  A. koreana 120
Abutilon 20-1
  A. megapotamicum 20, 20
  A. pictum 20
  A. vitifolium 20
Acanthopanax sieboldianus 21, 21
Acca sellowiana see Feijoa sellowiana
Acer 9, 22-5
  A. ginnala 22, 22
  A. japonicum 23, 23
  A. palmatum 23, 24-5, 24, 25
  A. shirazawanum 23
acid soils 13
alkaline soils 13
almond, flowering see Prunus triloba
Aloysia triphylla see Lippia citriodora
Amelanchier lamarckii 26, 26
angelica tree see Aralia elata
annuals 11
anthocyanins 8
aphids 16
Aralia elata 27, 27
Arctostaphylos uva-ursi 28, 28
Aronia arbutifolia 28-9, 29
Artemisia abrotanum 9, 29, 29
Atriplex halimus 30, 30
Aucuba japonica 30-1, 31

bamboo, sacred see Nandina domestica
bay, sweet see Laurus nobilis
bearberry see Arctostaphylos uva-ursi
beetles 16
bell heather see Erica cinerea
Berberis 8, 11, 32-5
  B. aggregata 34, 34
  B. atropurpurea 35

B. buxifolia 33
B. candidula 33
B. darwinii 33, 33
B. gagnepainii 33
B. julianae 32, 33, 33
B. linearifolia 32, 33
B. x lologensis 32, 33, 33
B. x media 33
B. x ottawensis 34
B. panianensis 33
B. x stenophylla 32, 33
B. thunbergii 34, 34, 35
B. verruculosa 33
B. vulgaris 34
B. wilsoniae 34
bilberry see Vaccinium
blackflies 16
blueberry see Vaccinium
box see Buxus
Brachyglottis see Senecio
broom, butcher's see Ruscus aculeatus
bulbs 11
Bupleurum fruticosum 36, 36
Buxus 9, 14, 36-7, 37
  B. microphylla 37
  B. sempervirens 37, 37

cabbage tree see Cordyline australis
Calluna vulgaris 38-9, 38, 39
Camellia 40, 40
  C. japonica 40
Caragana arborescens 40-1, 41
carotenoids 8
carpet bedding 6
Caryopteris x cladonensis 41, 41
castor oil plant see Fatsia japonica
caterpillars 16
Ceanothus 41
cedar see Cedrus
  Japanese see Cryptomeria japonica
  red see Thuja
Cedrus 123
Cephalotaxus 123
Ceratostigma 42
  C. plumbaginoides 42, 42
  C. willmottianum 42
Chamaecyparis 123

cherry, purple sand see Prunus x cistena
chlorophyll 8
Choisya ternata 43, 43
chokeberry see Aronia arbutifolia
cobnut see Corylus
Colletia 44
  C. hystrix 44
  C. paradoxa 44, 44
compost 12, 13
conifers 9, 120-5
Convolvulus cneorum 44-5
Cordyline australis 45, 45
Cornish heath see Erica vagans
Cornus 46-9
  C. alba 46, 46
  C. alternifolia 47, 47
  C. canadensis 48, 48
  C. controversa 48-9, 49
  C. florida 49, 49
Corylus 50
  C. avellana 50, 51
  C. laciniata 50
  C. maxima 50, 50
Corynabutilon see Abutilon vitifolium
Cotoneaster 52-5, 53
  C. adpressus 53
  C. atropurpureus 55
  C. bullatus 54, 55
  C. congestus 53
  C. conspicuus 53
  C. dammeri 53
  C. distichus 55
  C. divaricatus 54, 55, 55
  C. franchetii 53
  C. frigidus 52, 53
  C. horizontalis 54, 55, 55
  C. integrifolius 53
  C. lacteus 53
  C. microphyllus 53
  C. nanshan 53
  C. salicifolius 53, 53
  C. simonsii 54, 55
  C. thymifolius 53
  C. x watereri 53, 53
cranberry see Vaccinium
cross-leaved heath see Erica tetralix
Cryptomeria japonica 123
x Cupressocyparis 123
Cupressus 123
curry plant see

Helichrysum italicum
cuttings 15, 15
cypress see Cupressus
  false see Chamaecyparis
  Leyland see Cupressocyparis

Danaë racemosa 56, 56
Daphne 56-7
  D. x burkwoodii 57, 57
  D. laureola 56, 57
deciduous species 10, 11
Desfontainea spinosa 57, 57
Diervilla 58
  D. sessilifolia 58, 58
  D. x splendens 58
Disanthus cercidifolius 59, 59
diseases 16-19
dogwood see Cornus
Dorset heath see Erica ciliaris
Dorycnium hirsutum 60, 60
Drimys winteri 61, 61

Elaeagnus 62-3, 70
  E. angustifolia 63
  E. commutata 63
  E. x ebbingei 62, 62
  E. multiflora 63
  E. pungens 62, 62
  E. umbellata 63, 63
elder see Sambucus
Eleutherococcus see Acanthopanax sieboldianus
Enkianthus 64
  E. campanulatus 64, 64
  E. cernuus matsudae 64
  E. chinensis 64
Erica 65-8
  E. arborea 66, 67, 68
  E. carnea 65, 67, 68
  E. ciliaris 68
  E. cinerea 67, 68
  E. x darleyensis 66, 68
  E. erigena 68
  E. herbacea 68
  E. mediterranea 68
  E. tetralix 66, 67, 68
  E. vagans 66, 68
Eucryphia 69
  E. cordifolia 69
  E. glutinosa 69, 69

E. x nymansensis 69, 69
Euonymus 70-1
  E. alatus 71
  E. europaeus 70, 70, 71
  E. fortunei 70, 71, 71
  E. japonicus 70, 71
evergreen species 6, 10, 11

x Fatshedera lizei 72, 72
Fatsia 10, 10, 21
  F. japonica 72-3, 73
Feijoa sellowiana 73, 73
fertilizer 12
  deficiency 18
Ficus carica 74, 74
fig see Ficus carica
filbert see Corylus
flowering shrubs 10-11
Fothergilla 9
  F. gardenii 75
  F. major 75, 75
Fuchsia 76
  F. magellanica 76, 76
fungal diseases 16
fungicides 18-19

Griselinia littoralis 77, 77
guelder rose see Viburnum opulus

hazel see Corylus
heath see Erica
heather see Calluna vulgaris; Erica Hebe 11, 78
  H. x andersonii 78
  H. armstrongii 78
  H. cupressoides 78
  H. ochracea 78, 78
  H. pinguifolia 78, 78
  H. rakaiensis 78
  H. salicifolia 78
Hedera 18
  H. helix 79, 79
Helichrysum 80
  H. italicum 80
  H. petiolare (H. petiolatum) 80, 80
hemlock see Tsuga
herbaceous perennials 11
Hippophaë rhamnoides 81, 81
holly see Ilex
honeysuckle, bush see

Diervilla
Hydrangea quercifolia 82, 82

Ilex 9, 83
  I. aquifolium 83, 83
  I. crenata 83
insecticides 18-19
Itea ilicifolia 84, 84
ivy see *Hedera*

Japanese cowtail pine see *Cephalotaxus*
June berry see *Amelanchier lamarckii*
juniper see *Juniperus*
Juniperus 123-4
  J. communis 122
  J. horizontalis 121

kerosene weed see *Ozothamnus ledifolius*
Korean fir see *Abies*

lad's love see *Artemisia abrotanum*
larch see *Larix*
Larix 124
laurel 9
  Alexandrian see *Danaë racemosa*
  bay see *Laurus nobilis*
  cherry see *Prunus laurocerasus*
  Portugal see *Prunus lusitanica*
  spotted see *Aucuba japonica*
Laurus nobilis 84-5, 84
Lavandula 85
  L. angustifolia 85
  L. stoechas 85, 85
lavender see *Lavandula*
cotton see *Santolina*
layering 15
leaf spot 16
leaves
  colour, shape and size 8-9
  function 8
  glossy 9
  hairy 9
lemon verbena see *Lippia citriodora*
Leucothoë fontanesiana 86, 86

Ligustrum 86-7
  L. japonicum 86, 87
  L. lucidum 86, 87
  L. ovalifolium 86, 86, 87
Lippia citriodora 87, 87
Lomatia ferruginea 88, 88
Lonicera nitida 88-9, 89
Lotus hirsutus see *Dorycnium hirsutum*

Magnolia grandiflora 89, 89
Mahonia 90-1
  M. aquifolium 90, 90, 91
  M. x media 90, 90
manure 12, 13
Maple see *Acer*
Mediterranean heath see *Erica mediterranea*
Mexican orange blossom see *Choisya ternata*
mildew 16, 18
mineral deficiency 12
mixed borders 11
mock orange see *Philadelphus coronarius*
mulching 12-13
myrtle see *Myrtus communis*
Myrtus communis 91, 91

Nandina domestica 92, 92

oak-leaved hydrangea see *Hydrangea quercifolia*
Oregon grape see *Mahonia aquifolium*
Osmanthus 92-3
  O. x burkwoodii 93, 93
  O. decorus see *Phillyrea decora*
  O. heterophyllus 93
Ozothamnus 93
  O. ledifolius 93
  O. rosmarinifolius 93, 93

pea tree see *Caragana arborescens*
periwinkle see *Vinca*
pesticides 18-19
pests 16-19
pH scale 13
Philadelphus coronarius 94, 94
Phillyrea decora 94-5

Photinia x fraseri 95, 95
photosynthesis 8
Physocarpus opulifolius 96, 96
Picea 124
  P. pungens 125
Pieris 13, 96-7
  P. japonica 96, 97
pine see *Pinus*
pineapple guava see *Feijoa sellowiana*
Pinus 124
  P. strobus 125
Pittosporum tenuifolium 97, 97
plant names, meanings 122
Plumbago 42
privet 14
propagation 15, 15
pruning 14-15, 14
Prunus 98-100
  P. x cistena 98, 98
  P. laurocerasus 98-9, 99
  P. lusitanica 99, 99
  P. triloba 100, 100

Rhododendron 13, 101
  R. arboreum 101
  R. falconeri 101
  R. fulvum 101
  R. grande 101
  R. ponticum 101, 101
  R. sinogrande 9, 101
  R. yakushimanum 101

rosemary see *Rosmarinus officinalis*
Rosmarinus officinalis 9, 10, 102, 102
Rubus tricolor 102-3, 103
rue see *Ruta graveolens*
Ruscus aculeatus 103, 103
Russian olive see *Elaeagnus angustifolia*
rust 16
Ruta graveolens 9, 104, 104

Salix 104-5
  S. alba 105, 105
  S. x boydii 105
  S. exigua 105, 105
  S. gracilistyla 105
  S. lanata 105, 105
  S. magnifica 105

S. phylicifolia 105
S. purpurea 105
salt bush see *Atriplex halimus*
Sambucus 106
  S. nigra 106
  S. racemosa 106, 106
Santolina 107
  S. chamaecyparissus 107, 107
  S. pinnata neapolitana 107, 107
  S. virens 107
scale insects 16
sea buckthorn see *Hippophaë rhamnoides*
Senecio 108, 108
  S. greyi 108
  S. leucostachys 108
  S. viravira 108
shrubby germander see *Teucrium fruticans*
silver berry see *Elaeagnus commutata*
silver fir see *Abies*
Skimmia 108-9
  S. japonica 109
  S. laureola 109, 109
snowy mespilus see *Amelanchier lamarckii*
soil composition 13
Sophora tetraptera 109, 109
Sorbus reducta 9, 110, 110
specimen shrubs 10
spindle see *Euonymus europaeus*
Spiraea 110-11
  S. betulifolia 110, 111
  S. x bumalda 111
  S. japonica 110, 110, 111
  S. x vanhouttei 110, 111
spruce see *Picea*
Stephanandra incisa 111, 111
Symphoricarpos orbiculatus 112, 112

Taxus 124
Teucrium
  T. fruticans 112-13
  T. scorodonia 112
Thuja 124
  T. orientalis 125
topiary 36, 79, 99

tree heath see *Erica arborea*
Tsuga 124

Vaccinium 113
  V. arctostaphylos 113
  V. myrtillus 113, 113
variegated leaves 9
veronica see *Hebe*
Viburnum 16, 114-15
  V. acerifolium 114, 115
  V. alnifolium 115
  V. x bodnantense 114
  V. cylindricum 115
  V. davidii 115, 115
  V. furcatum 115
  V. x hillieri 114, 115
  V. lantanoides 115, 115
  V. opulus 114, 115
  V. "Pragense" 115
  V. rhytidophyllum 115, 115
  V. tinus 115
Vinca 116
  V. major 16, 116, 116
  V. minor 16, 116, 116
viral diseases 16

water loss 8, 9
wedding cake tree see *Cornus controversa*
Weigela florida 117
  W. 'Florida Variegata' 117
whiteflies 16
whortleberry, Caucasian see *Vaccinium arctostaphylos*
willow see *Salix*
winter's bark see *Drimys winteri*

Xanthoceras sorbifolium 118, 118

yew see *Taxus*
Yucca 10, 118-19
  Y. filamentosa 119
  Y. flaccida 119
  Y. gloriosa 119, 119

Zenobia pulverulenta 119, 119

PHOTOGRAPHIC ACKNOWLEDGEMENTS

Front cover: Andrew Lawson **Back cover**: Dr Stefan Buczacki

Inside photographs:

Amateur Gardening 92, 115 top left; Sue Atkinson 76, 97 top; Eric Crichton 6, 14 bottom, 20, 29 bottom, 42, 43, 45, 53 right, 63, 64, 65, 74, 85, 86 bottom, 89 top, 107 top, 113, 116 left, 122, 125 top right, 125 bottom right; John Glover 3, 24 left, 25 right, 34 bottom right, 37 left, 41 right, 67 top right, 67 top left, 84 bottom, 86 top; Derek Gould 58, 59, 71 left, 95, 105 bottom left, 110 bottom, 114 left, 115 bottom; Andrew Lawson 24 right, 27, 40, 49 top, 55 left, 56, 69 bottom, 73 bottom, 77, 78 top, 82, 94, 97 bottom, 105 top, 114 right, 116 right; Photos Horticultural 7, 8, 10, 11, 12, 14 top, 15 top, 15 bottom, 16, 21, 22, 23, 28, 30, 31, 32, 33 top right, 33 bottom left, 33 bottom right, 34 bottom left, 35, 36, 38, 39, 41 left, 47, 48, 49 bottom, 50, 51, 53 left, 55 right, 57 top, 57 bottom, 60, 61, 62 right, 66 left, 66 top right, 66 bottom right, 67 top centre, 67 bottom right, 69 top, 70, 71 top right, 71 bottom right, 72, 73 top, 75, 78 bottom, 80, 81, 83, 84 top, 87, 89 bottom, 90 left, 90 right, 91, 93 left, 96, 99 top, 101, 103 top, 108, 109 left, 110 top, 111 bottom, 112, 115 top right, 119 right, 121; Reed International Picture Library 46, 62 left, /Michael Boys 26; Harry Smith Collection 9, 13 top, 13 bottom, 18, 25 left, 29 top, 34 top right, 37 right, 44, 52, 54, 67 bottom right, 79 top, 79 bottom, 88, 93 right, 98, 99 bottom, 100, 102, 103 bottom, 104, 105 bottom right, 106, 107 bottom, 109 right, 111 top, 117, 118, 119 left, 120, 125 left.

TEMPERATURE CHART

BARELY HARDY	0 to -5°C	32 to 23°F
FAIRLY HARDY	-5 to -10°C	23 to 14°F
MODERATELY HARDY	-10 to -15°C	14 to 5°F
HARDY	-15 to -20°C	5 to -4°F
VERY HARDY	-20°C or below	-4°F or below